Becoming a

TRUE
SPIRITUAL
COMMUNITY

*A Profound Vision of What
the Church Can Be*

LARRY CRABB

THOMAS NELSON
Since 1798

NASHVILLE DALLAS MEXICO CITY RIO DE JANEIRO BEIJING

Published in Nashville, TN, by Thomas Nelson. Thomas Nelson is a trademark of Thomas Nelson, Inc.

Thomas Nelson, Inc. titles may be purchased in bulk for educational, business, fund-raising, or sales promotional use. For information, please e-mail SpecialMarkets @ThomasNelson.com.

Scripture quotations noted NIV are from the HOLY BIBLE: NEW INTERNATIONAL VERSION ®. © 1973, 1978, 1984, by International Bible Society. Used by permission of Zondervan Publishing House. All rights reserved.

Scripture quotations noted NKJV are from THE NEW KING JAMES VERSION. © 1979, 1980, 1982, Thomas Nelson, Inc., Publishers.

Library of Congress Cataloging-in-Publication Data

Crabb, Lawrence J.
    The safest place on earth : where people connect and are forever changed / Larry Crabb.
        p. cm.
    Includes bibliographical references.
    ISBN-10: 0-8499-1456-6 (hard cover)
    ISBN-13: 978-0-8499-1456-0 (hard cover)
    ISBN-10: 0-8499-1884-7 (trade paper)
    ISBN-13: 978-0-8499-1884-1 (trade paper)
    1. Christian communities. 2. Spiritual life—Christianity. I. Title.
    BV4405.C73
    262'26—dc21   99-38663
                                                                   CIP

Printed in the United States of America
13 14 15 QG 9 8 7 6 5 4

CONTENTS

Part III
A Way of Relating in This World

To my spiritual community.
Let's keep on journeying to God—together

FOREWORD

Most of us assume that having decided to follow Jesus as our Lord and Savior we will find ourselves in a spiritual community of like-minded friends, a family of brothers and sisters, enjoying one another's companionship on our way to glory.

More often than not we are disappointed. Why? Why is spiritual community—"church"—high on so many people's list as a major spiritual problem?

The question is no respecter of persons: young and old, men and women in the pews and pastors in their pulpits, long-time Christians, new Christians, and not-quite-yet Christians. The question ranges across denominational lines. The question is spoken variously in loud anger, in mocking cynicism, and in hardly audible despair. Predictably, in a demand-supply spiritual economy, answers come pouring in.

Larry Crabb, unpredictably, doesn't answer the question.

Instead, he invites us into an extended, leisurely conversation on the emphatically personal and inter-personal nature of all human life, sharply focused in the trinitarian revelation of this life in Jesus. He immerses us in the centrality of spiritual community (or church) as Christ is formed in us (Gal. 4:19) and we grow up to "the full stature of Christ" (Eph. 4:13)—we can't do this by ourselves; individualism is not an option. And he insists—this may be the most important thing he does for us—on embracing the formidable difficulties involved in spiritual community: there are no instant intimacies in this business; there are no shortcuts; there is no avoiding confusion and disappointment. We had better be ready for a lifelong process of demanding ventures in following Jesus into the company of the broken men and women who are also hurrying or hobbling after him.

The honesty and urgency that characterize these pages is a welcome contrast to the prevailing entrepreneurial spirit of our age that turns community into a commodity. Community impoverished Christians are ripe for such exploitation. Our need for community and our dissatisfaction with the community we are in (or looking over) provides a wide open field for the men and women who are selling "community." Community as commodity is one of the more spectacular growth industries in North American religion today. How does it happen that what originates as a creation of the Holy Spirit so frequently (and so lucratively!) gets packaged as a technique or a product?

What is being sold, on inspection doesn't turn out to be community at all. Americans are good at forming clubs and gathering crowds. But clubs and crowds, even when—especially when—they are religious clubs and crowds, are not communities. The formation of community is the intricate, patient, painful work of the Holy Spirit. We cannot buy or make community; we can only offer ourselves to become community. By turning away from the managerial and leadership skills that are held in such high regard in our culture, and returning us to the actual conditions in which true spiritual communities develop, *Becoming a True Spiritual Community* provides us instruction and wisdom and hope to re-enter the places we have been given and the people we find there, ready to be formed by the Word and Spirit of God into spiritual community.

Eugene H. Peterson
Professor Emeritus of Spiritual Theology
Regent College

ACKNOWLEDGMENTS

This book marks a sort of milestone for me. It's the first one I've written without soliciting feedback during the process. No one but Claudia saw a single sentence till it was completed.

Before, I think I felt a little afraid to express what was most passionate within me. Marcia, an accomplished artist and a true spiritual friend, suggested that feedback during creative work can be double-edged: you may get a better sense of how people will hear and evaluate what you're saying but that sense will likely alter at least some of what comes out of you onto a canvas or page.

The result was extra struggle. Being is so much tougher than performing. What you're about to read went through four or five false starts, each several chapters long, before my spirit felt engaged with His. As I holed up in several hotel rooms for a few weeks of intensive writing and hid in my basement office over the course of a year, I prayed my way into a conscious sense of God's presence. Then, standing on the shoulders of so many, I wrote what the Spirit opened my eyes to see and my heart to say.

Without Claudia Ingram, this book would likely be a bunch of disorganized scribbles on note paper in a file somewhere. Not only her ability to read faxed handwriting and produce a neat manuscript but far more her fierce, loyal passion to see God get whatever mileage He can out of me is an ongoing source of single-edged influence—all good.

Joey Paul, my main man at W Publishing Group, has poured something of himself into this book. More than a publisher, he is a friend and co-laborer in kingdom work. To the entire W Publishing Group team, a big thanks for believing in this project.

Lela Gilbert edited the manuscript into a far more readable book. Lisa Guest digested my ideas well enough to come up with excellent study questions. My thanks to both.

Sealy Yates lacks the grace to let me win on the golf course, but his singular passion for God and His people inflames everything he does as we work closely together. The term *literary agent* fails to convey how wonderfully his involvement stirs my passion for Christ.

Jerry Miller arouses boldness within me to tell whatever God has told me. Frank Wilson pours something alive in him into me every time we connect. Chuck Yeager's ability to cut to the chase has helped me focus on what my message really is.

Jim and Suzi Kallam, Dwight and Sandy Edwards, Trip and Judy Moore, and Kent and Karla Denlinger are pastor/couple friends who define for Rachael and me the term *spiritual friendship*. Our love runs deep.

Enormous thanks to my prayer team who prayed on a given day every week as I wrote this book. Randy and Marcia, Kep and Kim, Richard, Phoebe, Duncan and Angie, Al and Jeanie, Freddie and Sarah, Kent and Karla, Bill and Sandy, Frank and Chris, Christine, Wes and Judy, Ken, Curtis, Bill and Mary, Tom and Jenny, Margaret, Monte and Cheryl, Chuck, Bob and Claudia, Anthony and Diane, Jim and Suzi. Whatever spiritual wisdom is in these pages is the direct result of your faithful labor.

So many others were used to awaken my hunger for intimacy with God and others: Ron and Jenny, Mark, Elisa and Evan, Philip and Janet, Ken and Diane, Chap and Dee, Tom and Vickey, George and Connie, Mike and Julianne, and scores of others. Thank you.

To my sons: your walk with God puts joy in my heart that can come from nowhere else. To my parents: your clinging to God during severe trial has empowered me to do the same during my dark nights.

And to my wife: you have paid the highest price of any for whatever work the Spirit is doing in me and through me. Thank you for knitting your heart with mine as together we journey toward the light ahead. The word *together* brings tears to my eyes. Together is God's design.

INTRODUCTION

Let's Turn
Our Chairs

It was a sight I can't forget. I've tried. In the twenty-five years that have passed since I saw it, only a few details have blurred. The broad features of that scene, and most of the specifics, remain as clear in my memory as if I had witnessed it yesterday.

Rachael and I were touring Miami Beach. We had recently moved to South Florida from the gray Midwest and were enjoying our first chance to visit the famed sunshine vacation paradise.

One block west of the luxury beach hotels—the ones pictured on all the postcards—was a very ordinary big-city street, noisy, dirty, heavily trafficked with cabs and buses and plumbing repair trucks. The street was lined with less-than-elegant businesses and shops and row dwellings, with the occasional green shrub poking its way out of a square foot of dirt in the concrete. A patch of blue sky was visible only if you looked straight up.

No one was snapping pictures to send home or put in scrapbooks. At one point, we walked in front of a wood-slatted porch, maybe ten feet deep, with perhaps sixty feet of sidewalk frontage. At least a hundred chairs were arranged in neat rows and columns, none touching, each in exactly the same position to the others.

The occupied chairs (and most of them were) each held one motionless retired man or woman staring straight ahead at the street. I can't recall seeing anyone rocking, though I'm sure someone was. I do remember that no heads turned to follow a passing taxi or pedestrian, or to chat with another porch-sitter. I didn't see any crossed legs (I remember one woman's stockings were bunched around her ankles). There were no paperback novels or newspapers, not even a cup of coffee or a glass of iced tea. There was no conversation, no evidence that any of these people had been created by a relational God to enjoy intimate relating.

These people's souls were asleep, numbed, I suppose, by years of lifeless relationships and pointless conversations. No doubt those conversations had all seemed important at the time—business deals, romantic encounters, child scoldings, religious meetings—but maybe such encounters with other people had never touched anything deep enough to stir life.

I remember thinking, *All their lives everyone on this porch worked hard in Detroit or New York with the dream of retiring in Florida. And now they've made it. But look at them! Everything they've lived for has come to this. Lord, deliver me from living in a manner that will leave me one day sitting in a chair next to other people who are also sitting in chairs looking straight ahead, never into another person's eyes, never knowing anyone, and known by no one.*

The sight of that porch was unspeakably sad. I can't forget it. As we walked by, my wife whispered to me (I'm not sure why she whispered, since no one was listening), "I feel this strange urge to break into a dance and start singing at the top of my lungs."

It's a similar urge that prompts me to write this book.

I wonder if the Spirit feels as we did when He walks by a group of Christians. There are, of course, some differences. Most often we're chatting, sometimes singing, occasionally (in certain circles) dancing. We're engaging in serious conversations, Bible study, storytelling, and weekend retreat planning, as well as in lively but mundane interactions about sports and juicy "did-you-hear-about-so-and-so" tidbits.

Every Sunday morning we stand, then sit, then sing on command. Some of us raise our hands, most of us sit still while someone talks to us. At some point we reach into our wallets and drop a mixture of green and silver into a big soup bowl with a velvet lining to keep the silver from clanging.

We're *doing* a lot. But I wonder if the Spirit, who lives in a circle with two Others who are always *relating*, sees us as Rachael and I saw the retired folks on the Miami Beach porch: lined up in chairs facing straight ahead with no life passing back and forth among them. Is that what we really look like?

A pastor who ministers to small groups in a sizable church recently told me, "People in our home fellowships do what the manuals instruct them to do. They tell personal stories, share prayer requests, discuss interesting things, reflect on biblical texts, worship together, sometimes even weep for one another. But something's not going on that should be, something everyone wants. I don't know what it is, but it's missing."

Even when a few of us gather together to relate, do we somehow manage to keep our souls to ourselves, never really *meeting*, neither giving nor receiving what is most wanted?

Another small group pastor said to me over lunch, "We've got to move to another level. Good things are happening in our groups, but not what most needs to happen, not what I somehow know *could* happen."

Then she reminded me of Miami Beach. She said, "We arrange our bodies in a circle, but our souls are sitting in straight-backed chairs facing away from the others. We all play it safe because none of us feel safe in the group—not really."

I'm writing this book because I want to see us turn our chairs. Our souls need to face each other. And then I want us to get off our chairs and onto our knees. Before we climb back up to our seats, I want us to wash each other's feet, maybe figuratively, maybe literally.

Worship, humility, *then* dialogue. That's the order.

Then I want us to talk with each other, not merely to make conversation, but to make a difference, to be caught up in another sphere, the world of the Spirit, where first things are first and second things are second. I want us to experience a kind of oneness that makes us aware of what's best inside us and of all the bad stuff that blocks its release, a *penetrating* oneness that releases nice little boys to be men and sweet little girls to be women.

I think that's what the writer to the Hebrews had in mind. He told us to never stop getting together with other Christians. And, when we do get together, to say and do things that stir a flame into a fire, to arouse the life God's Spirit has placed within us so we can go on through dark nights or pleasant mornings with our eyes fixed on unseen reality. He told us to consider, to *think hard*, about what all that means.

But that's not what we've done. Instead, we've found ways to "do church," even to participate in small groups that don't require real connecting, ways to involve ourselves with fellow Christians without fully turning our chairs. We've walked well-traveled roads, broad highways involving activity, organization, and ambition (both secular and religious), and built church buildings along the way. We've welcomed into our buildings the throngs of travelers who walk those roads with us and herded them into audiences we call communities.

But they're nothing of the sort. In real community people know each other; they relate in ways only God's Spirit makes possible. As a friend recently commented, "I worship so much better when I'm with people I know." Christians in community give and receive what God provides through no other means than through a handful of folks who intimately know Him and each other or who at least are in passionate pursuit of that goal.

Churches are rarely communities. More often they are social machines that run smoothly for a while, break down, then are fixed so they run smoothly again or noisily chug along as best they can. The invitation to greet pew mates during the early part of the worship service typically leads nowhere. It's often nothing more than a squirt of oil on the gears. You could state your name was Bob or Howard or Rita or Sue and it would make no difference. Those kinds of interactions rarely create community—they more often substitute for it.

The path of the Spirit is so very different. It's narrower, steeper, and straighter than any other. It's a path traveled only by worshippers who celebrate their dependence on God and each other by turning their chairs toward a small community of friends and sticking with them, and who find the power of God's Spirit to make that community work. They know that God gives them His Spirit and works miracles both in them and among them, not because they cleverly make it happen, but because they revel in their dependence and learn to hear the Spirit's voice (see Galatians 3:5).

There are many paths through life, some well traveled, some that attract only a few pilgrims, but there is only one that leads to true community, to the safest place on earth where souls connect and are forever changed.

We're told to think hard about that path and where it takes us.

That's what I want to do in this book.

My plan is to write about *spiritual community*. I want to talk about what it might mean for us to turn our chairs toward each other and pour out the life in our hearts into our brothers and sisters, and to let them pour into us. It is sometimes more difficult to receive than to give. In spiritual communities, people do both.

Part I describes *a way of thinking about spiritual community*. What is it? How can we relate to each other in ways that require the Spirit, in ways non-Christians never can? What would attract them and make them curious? People without the Spirit often get along quite well (not every good neighbor is a Christian), and some of them perform deeds of inspiring sacrifice and rich kindness. What makes a *spiritual* community unique?

In Part II, I develop *a way of understanding our struggles* that makes it clear why spiritual friends and spiritual directors—the two major kinds of relationships in spiritual community—are best suited to help us. Spiritual community is a safer place than professional community, though for many the opposite has proved true. (However, when spiritual community is unsafe, it really isn't spiritual.)

Finally, in Part III, I offer the nuts and bolts of my message, *a way of relating in this world* that defines what it means to be in spiritual community.

And that requires us to turn our chairs.

PART I

A Way of
Thinking about
Spiritual Community

CHAPTER 1

For God's Sake,
Don't Expect It to Be Easy

*I ponder my experience and I recognize once more that the
way for us to be in the world is to focus on the
spiritual life.*—Henri Nouwen

Every Christian effort to think through what it takes to personally change necessarily involves some level of confusion and disappointment. And for good reason. Every Christian effort to actually change, especially with the help of people, is at times confusing and disappointing.

The journey toward Christ is not easily mapped. Whatever map we come up with will be less than precise, and sincere attempts to follow it will not lead to a bump-free existence.

Christian living, in some measure, and in some seasons more acutely than others, will always bewilder and frustrate us. As we sort through our ideas about Christian counseling and the church, as we debate the differences between therapy, spiritual direction, lay counseling, and discipleship, we really should admit that we don't quite know what we're talking about. Neither the goal toward which we're aiming (exactly what does it mean to be whole, to be mature?) nor the process of getting there is clearly understood by anyone.

What do we do with the young man who gets furious when a woman won't date him? How should we respond when a relationship cools and tensions surface? Should we talk about it and try to understand what's happening, or is it best to cover the problem with renewed efforts to love? We don't always know.

What does maturity look like a week after your husband leaves you or two days after you lose your job? Does it look different in different people? What are the constants? How do spiritually committed folks handle it when memories of terrible abuse come back, or when a good friend betrays them? What do we do with the sleep-robbing doubt that plagues most honest people in their journey toward faith? And are we certain how to encourage whatever it is we're after? How do you talk with a woman who keeps switching personalities or a man who binges and purges on pornography?

What are we trying to achieve and how do we think we'll get there? When we move beyond simply wanting people to show up for church, to support the budget, and to do nothing publicly immoral or disruptive, when we enter people's lives and see what the inside struggles are, we feel confused. And often disappointed.

In the midst of all our efforts to describe the spiritual life, to live it, and to help others live it, there are some things we simply don't know. Paul and John taught that none of us (including them) can see exactly what true maturity looks like (1 Cor. 13:12; 1 John 3:2–3). And we won't see clearly until we lay our eyes on Christ. Only then will we know. Only then, after gazing on Him for a thousand years (it will seem like a day), will we look in a mirror and, with both astonishment and strange recognition, cry out, "So *that's* what Christian maturity looks like. Of course!" Until then, we should expect to grope a bit, to know we're always wrong about a few things, and to change our minds more than once. We should hold many convictions, some firmly, and only a few dogmatically.

Confusion isn't always a bad thing. If we're not confused about anything it's likely we're grasping the truth about nothing important. Developing convictions about vital matters is never easy and, until heaven, is an ongoing, never finished process.

Beware, then, the guru, no matter how well pedigreed, with a complete system that explains personal problems fully and tells Christian helpers exactly what to do. Confusion need not be nourished—and about some basics it need not exist—but it should be expected, even welcomed, as we explore what it means to live spiritually in an unspiritual world, or in Nouwen's words, to focus on the spiritual life.

Disappointment, too, is inevitable. More than that, it is good. Following Christ *must* take us through seasons of disappointment, because Christianity remakes our dreams before it fulfills them. The process is excruciating. It can include divorce, bankruptcy, accidents, murder, near apostasy—anything.

However, insisting that all spiritual people will suffer, I must point out, is *not* the same thing as insisting that happiness should not be our concern. I believe it should. I can't quite see valuing unhappiness. And I certainly wouldn't follow someone who promised only to make me miserable. In fact, a sensible theology of suffering *affirms* our desire to be happy.

What I am saying is that our ideas about happiness need a major overhaul, and that only the suffering brought about by shattered dreams can do the job. Although our yearnings to feel happy are good, we're in for some rude surprises if we follow the Christian path toward their satisfaction.

Christianity promises happiness—that's part of its appeal—but we will not find it by traveling the route we've already laid out in our heads. Disappointment, severe enough to be called death, is unavoidable in a true spiritual journey. As Dennis the Menace once told his pal Joey, "Mr. Wilson says that if you want to give God a good laugh, tell Him your future plans."

The upside of confusion is openness. Confused people listen better, not always, but more often than people whose minds are made up. Those folks listen only in order to critique, to see if someone else is on the right track, namely theirs. Confused people are more likely to combine kindness with whatever convictions emerge out of their confusion. And, because of their eagerness for meaningful dialogue with honest people, the convictions they develop tend to speak to the realities of life as it really is lived.

Disappointment has an upside as well. It inspires hope by making hope necessary. And the hope it inspires need not be the soul-numbing opiate Marxists warn against, or the wish-fulfilling fantasies that Freudians interpret away.

Once you grant the unconfusing and thoroughly nondisappointing fact that Christ's atonement guarantees the Spirit's ceaseless work in our lives—from conception through death and on into eternity—then disappointment brings forth better dreams, the longing for a larger hope, without which we are intolerably miserable. Soul-crushing struggle supplies the energy that nudges us along in the process of shifting from *token hope*, the kind that generates pleasant feelings, to the *real thing* that anchors us through life's storms.

As I begin another book, this one presenting my developing views on the largely untapped power of spiritual community to change lives, I am personally aware of both confusion and disappointment. I'm confused about the exact kind of relationship that heals someone's soul and about how it does its work. I have plenty of thoughts and several convictions, but only a little part of the picture feels nailed down in my mind.

And I'm disappointed, overwhelmingly so, when I take stock of the current state of Christian community. In my own life, there are several bright pockets of relational joy, for which I am extremely grateful, but none that quite measure up to Trinitarian standards.

Both the confusion and disappointment are, I think, doing their work. I feel more *open* than ever to moving wherever the Spirit directs, and I am strongly *hopeful* that He will lead God's people, including me, into a deeper experience of spiritual community.

About some things I am not confused. The essentials of the Christian faith, what Lewis called "mere Christianity," I gladly affirm to be true.[1] About some other things, like psychology's value, whether counseling is legitimate, and whether the Bible tells us how to counsel, there are many opinions. Perhaps a few brief statements indicating my views on these hot topics will provide a framework for presenting my thoughts about the healing power of safe community.

• *Is psychology good or bad?*

For guiding the church in providing soul care, I grant neither an authoritative nor a supplemental role to the discipline of psychology. I believe that empirical science and theoretical speculation must yield to special revelation and biblically dependent thinking in building a foundation and coming up with a strategy for this all-important work.

But I do acknowledge that observation and inference about human behavior can stimulate our thinking. It can serve a legitimate catalytic function, even when done by unregenerate psychologists. Good exegetes of Scripture read widely not only to critique but also to think. Psychology bashers who study only their Bibles and read the works of psychologists with disdain, tend to approach neither with the humility appropriate to struggling seekers. They often end up with a moralistic version of soul care that misses the relational thrust of the Bible.

• *Do Christians need counseling?*

Talking about problems in a caring, open relationship with a discerning counselor is a good thing to do. What makes a counselor good, what makes for good counseling, and where and by whom and on what schedule counseling is best done are other questions.

• *Can you talk about deep personal longings without encouraging a need-centered approach to helping people?*

I reject a need-centered, anthropocentric understanding of human nature. I do not believe (and never have) that anyone should devote himself or herself to gaining a sense of personal security and significance before they get around to obeying God and loving others.

We are already secure and significant in Christ. Our sins have been forgiven and we've been called and equipped to advance His kingdom. We have what we need to do what we should do. No one can rightly plead poor self-esteem or a damaging background or difficult circumstances as an excuse for ungodly living. But it is still true that we were built for relationship and that we long for the intimacy true relationship provides.

- *Does building up the body of Christ mean we only affirm what is good in people and never confront sin?*

Disruption has its place. Facing one's sin and pain, continually but never obsessively or centrally, is part of the spiritual journey. Subtleties of both, what I call *flesh dynamics,* are sometimes best recognized by seasoned, discerning counselors.

- *How important is the Christian community in helping people deal with their problems?*

I am radically pro-community. I believe that under the terms of God's New Covenant with humankind, the Holy Spirit has graciously placed resources in every Christian that, when released from one person and received into another, can promote substantial healing and change. A *connecting* community, where each member is joined together in dynamic spiritual union, is a *healing* community.

- *Is the Bible a counseling textbook, or must we look elsewhere for guidance in how to counsel?*

I believe in the Bible's authority and sufficiency for the work of counseling. In my mind, authority and sufficiency aren't the troubling questions. Our trouble begins with hermeneutics. Of course the Bible is both true and sufficient, but how do we use it? That's the burning question.

A scholastic approach to Bible study, which seeks to master the text and to articulate its truths and principles, often arrives at a prescriptive style of counseling: Believe this and do that! The relationship between counselor and counselee (or pastor and congregation) is not the focus. Community, which the Bible reveals as central to life, becomes a side issue while biblical accuracy and strict application become the exclusive focus.

The therapeutic culture has reacted against that hermeneutic (and its result) by advocating an integration model: (1) Integrate whatever Scriptures are relevant to counseling issues with (2) good psychological insights that don't contradict Scripture and you will come up with a Christian approach to counseling. An integration model denies, if not biblical authority, at least biblical sufficiency.

I vote for a third option, neither moralism, nor integration-based therapy, but rather a communitarian model. This approach emerges from a hermeneutic of well-informed subjectivism:[2] Study the text not only as a good scholar but also as an honest struggler.

First, ask what questions God has bothered to answer in the Word. Only He is wise enough to know which questions need answering. Then study His answers for the rest of your life.

Second, as study continues, bring to what you're learning the questions that honest living requires you to ask. And assume (this is important) that in the community of faith where the Bible is trusted, you will find all you need to know to live as you were re-created to live. The result, I believe, will be neither prescriptive counseling nor therapeutic counseling but rather communitarian counseling—an approach rooted in deep respect for the power of God's Spirit to change lives through spiritual community.

- *The church and Scripture have an obvious role to play in dealing with spiritual problems. But what about psychological problems? Don't they require expert professional care?*

There is no meaningful distinction between psychological and spiritual problems, only between physical and personal problems. (Even there, the distinction is sometimes fuzzy.)

Personal problems require personal care, or *pastoral* care. I do not use this term to imply that only pastors should counsel. I use it to suggest that soul care can best be provided within spiritual community. Psychotherapy, when it is seen as something other than soul care, is illegitimate. Only soul care, richly defined, is needed for personal problems, whether we call them psychological or spiritual.

- *Can soul care at the deepest level really happen in a local church?*

Soul care requires two kinds of relationships: spiritual friendship and spiritual direction. Both exist only as part of spiritual community. Neither is common in the Western church.

Rather than thinking in terms of therapists, counselors, pastoral counselors, and lay counselors, I propose thinking of a healing community as providing two kinds of relationships: *spiritual friendship*, which exists among spiritually minded peers who share their lives together, and *spiritual direction*, which takes place when time is specially set aside for one person to present his or her life to a respected (not always familiar) person who agrees to listen, pray, think, and speak, preferably without pay.

This book is really a discussion of the idea that spiritual community is far more powerful than we've assumed. In my view it is a much-needed discussion because good conversations among spiritual friends and with a spiritual director are uncommon in our church communities.

We don't need more churches, as we usually define the word. We need more *spiritual communities* where good friends and wise people turn their chairs toward each other and talk well. Developing them will not be easy. As you read my ideas, even if you should agree with everything I say, some confusion will remain. That's how it must be. That's how it *should* be.

And if a group of Christians were to use this book to guide their efforts in actually building community, they would run into significant disappointment. That can't be helped. Confusion and disappointment will be our companions till heaven, no matter whose ideas we follow. Things will be different then, but until we get there, let's think hard about what spiritual community could be now.

CHAPTER 2

It's Not Easy,
but It's Worth It

If the church has a future it is a future with the poor in
whatever form.—Henri Nouwen

In the LORD I take refuge. How then can you say to me:
"Flee like a bird to your mountain. . . . When the foundations
are being destroyed, what can the righteous do?"—Psalm 11:1, 3 NIV

W e need each other, never more than when we are most broken. But
brokenness is not a disease, like cancer, that may or may not develop.
Brokenness is a condition, one that is always there, inside, beneath the surface, carefully hidden for as long as we can keep a facade in place. We live
in brokenness. We just don't always see it, either in ourselves or in others.

A central task of community is to create a place that is safe enough
for the walls to be torn down, safe enough for each of us to own and
reveal our brokenness. Only then can the power of connecting do its job.
Only then can community be used of God to restore our souls.

When we turn our chairs to face each other, the first thing we see
is a terrible fact: We're all struggling. Beneath the surface of every

personality—even the one that seems most "together"—a spiritual battle is raging that will only be won with the help of community. Think with me about the nature of that battle and what kind of community might help.

It is in the nature of things that our natural foundations must be destroyed if true spirituality is to develop. There is no other way, although I wish there were. Perhaps that is why, in His bewildering mercy, God sometimes shatters our fondest dreams, or at least allows them to be shattered. (Whether He is the cause or merely allows it to happen, the result is the same. And in the midst of the pain, the distinction doesn't always seem important.)

In His sovereignly run universe, the unthinkable sometimes happens—the nightmare we thought we'd never have to face. And no relief comes, sometimes not for years. More frequently than untested Christians expect, God removes the one source of joy and meaning that we were counting on to make our lives worth living, and replaces it with nothing.

As I write these words, national television continues to show the scenes of horror that in April 1999 took place in Littleton, Colorado, less than ten miles from where I live. Thirteen families lost sons or daughters, victims of the shooting rampage of two teenage boys. The boys' families bear not only the grief of their sons' double suicide, but the tumult and chaos of their unexplained violence.

The foundations of assumed safety, of at least some sense of predictability and fairness, of happy family life, have all been destroyed in one morning of heartless carnage. And people pray. They turn to God.

For what? To raise our dead? To give us comfort? To explain why He allows this one to die and that one to live?

When my brother died in a plane crash, one speaker at the memorial service said this: "Don't be afraid to ask the hardest questions that rise up in your soul. But don't expect answers. Expect rather to experience God." But that doesn't always happen, at least not right away, and perhaps not in the form we think it should.

Without compromising His love and good purposes, which we try hard to believe He cannot and will not do, God puts us in a box where all we have is Him. I think it was Tozer who once compared a man complaining that all he had left was God to a fish bemoaning that all it had left was the ocean. The point is well taken, but the problem with enjoying it is that God sometimes seems more like a picture of the ocean on a travel brochure than the real thing. And you can't swim in a picture.

Something is happening in the Western church. More of us are becoming aware of a deep hunger for a new kind of worship, for relating in new ways to each other. A friend told me just yesterday: "I feel so heavy every time I walk out of church. My burden doesn't lift. It gets heavier. I just want to talk to God and hear Him talk to me. And I want to talk to a few friends."

I write this book to my many fellow pilgrims whose foundations are cracking or perhaps are already destroyed. You're tired. Life isn't turning out as you'd expected. When you became a Christian, you packed your bags for Bermuda but your plane landed in Iceland. Without a coat, you need the warmth of community to survive.

You thought by now you'd be farther ahead spiritually, less tempted toward bad things like pornography or despair, more content in a church fellowship, better connected to family and friends. You expected, after all those years in church and mornings with your Bible, to struggle less with spiritual dryness, greed, loneliness, and anger; to be happier in career and ministry, more optimistic and relaxed.

After all, you've been at this thing called the Christian life for quite some time. Like Peter, you tell the Lord that you've been working hard all night and haven't caught a thing. And He says, "Let down the nets. Row back into deep water."

It doesn't seem reasonable. You've tried before, in the same lake. The fish aren't there.

Perhaps your foundations haven't slowly eroded. Maybe they've suddenly blown up. And you're right now reeling from aftershock. Ministry efforts you *knew* were directed by God have failed or become mired in endless complications. You're deeply discouraged. Nothing matters much. The "oomph" to go on is gone.

Perhaps divorce has introduced a new kind of pain, a kind you'd never before experienced and never thought you would. It's worse than all the descriptions you'd heard. Your choices are to stay mad, to make yourself numb, or to go crazy. And a fourth option—pleasurable sin—has renewed appeal.

A diagnosis of cancer demands more trust than you can find within yourself. Every morning when you awake, your first thought is, *I have cancer,* or *Will it return?* Clouds always block the sun. Your world is gray.

Then the questions come: "Who is this God I claim to love? Where is He? I know He's good, but what good is He? Sometimes I think I hate Him." Hating can seem so reasonable, so stabilizing, so life-giving, so mature.

More questions arise: "Will He ever show up? Will I ever feel His love to the point where a passion for His glory exceeds my passion for relief? Will He ever make just one thing go right, or cause something to make sense?" As one friend put it after a series of particularly severe trials, "Couldn't God get glory by just once doing what I want Him to do?"

You ask another question, and another: "Who am I? They tell me I'm someone special, loved, chosen before the foundation of the world, a friend of God. If this is the way He treats His friends, maybe being His enemy wouldn't be so bad. What difference does it make? What difference does anything make? My husband is sick. I can't pay my bills. My mother has Alzheimer's—she doesn't even know my name. The only reason I can think of to believe the gospel is to avoid hell. Sometimes I feel I'm already there. Just exactly what is God doing for me now?"

You cry out to God. There is no answer.

I was praying for a friend yesterday. The image that came to my mind as I prayed was of a lone figure standing in a deserted field at night, raising his fist to God and shouting, "Where are You? My soul is dying. My life is in shreds. And You do nothing! Why won't You talk to me?"

In my image, I walked up to him and embraced him. We talked; he wept as he poured out his heart. But soon I had to leave. He yelled at me as I walked away, "I thought you were my friend. And now you're walking away, too, leaving me alone. I'm angry, and you don't care!"

As I continued to move away from him, I looked back and saw him once again standing alone, his fist raised toward God, shouting words that I could no longer hear. I was tempted to rush back to him, but I didn't. I sensed that at this time in his journey the gift of my absence was better than the gift of my presence. Or, perhaps I should have stayed longer with my friend. I'm not sure. How should we "be there" for each other? It's sometimes hard to know.

When I describe the experience of cracked or destroyed foundations, I believe I am describing the experience of every pilgrim who honestly pursues the Lord. The path to the joy of God's presence always leads through joyless isolation, when the part of us that most longs for connection is left painfully alone.

When that happens, and when we cry out in pain, the nature of our spiritual community is revealed.

Some people, often our leaders and close friends, communicate disgusted impatience and disrespect: "Get over it! Stop whining! Stop feeling sorry for yourself and do something for someone else!"

Others respond more in the spirit of our day. They see our pain, at least some of it, and try to help: "See a counselor. Try medication. Go ahead and express your real feelings. Practice the spiritual disciplines. Or maybe you should get away for a couple of days."

These folks mean well, but you can't help but feel irritated, pressured, and strangely dishonored. If you're like me, you feel most annoyed when, uninvited, someone tries to "counsel" you, to explore your background or say something wise.

I recently spoke about where I am on my spiritual journey with part of my community—a Sunday school class of about fifty people. It felt like a huge risk; I didn't feel safe. My most intense fear was that someone would try to *help* me. Instead, I longed for my friends to enter my world, to be intrigued with what God was doing in my life, to ask questions, to honor my place in the journey, and to do it all with no agenda. I didn't want them to offer what our therapy-mad culture thinks is helpful: to look for pathology that can be treated; to find something wrong that can be fixed.

I told them I was more aware than ever of how much *self* is mixed up in all that I do. When I speak, I worry over how well I'll do, how I'll be received. I want to give whatever God has given me with His glory uppermost in mind. But a passion for my own glory always sneaks in. I can *feel* it.

As I shared all this in a way that for me seemed new, I felt ugly. I feared both their withdrawal and their correction. But I feared cosmetic help even more: "If you just do this or that, you'd be a lot more attractive." The *effort* to help seems often like a *demand* to help. And it can feel so condescending.

An excerpt from Henri Nouwen's journal, written in the last year of his life, gave me the courage to say something more.[1] After acknowledging my woundedness, how the wrong comment, a single look, one piece of bad news can throw me into an instant funk of insecure and angry neediness, I said—and this is the part that required courage—that I don't expect the wounds to ever heal till I reach heaven. Nouwen came to the same conclusion in his last year of life.

I have given up on healing, if healing means a repair job on what is wrong inside me that will lessen my struggles. I am now searching for a path to maturity that doesn't focus so intensely on all that's wrong with me, on all the unsatisfied longings of my heart that seem to require a self-protective style of relating, on whatever traumatic memories still sting.

That was followed, in my remarks to the class, by a few excerpts from *The Story of a Soul,* the extraordinary record of how God worked in the life of St. Theresa of Lisieux, a nun who died at age twenty-four in 1897.[2] As I read of her remarkable affection for Christ and a devotion to Him that actually grew during seasons of joylessness, I felt alive with hope. "This could be my story," I told the class. "I'm not there now, but what the Spirit did for St. Theresa, He could do for this unsaintly saint."

I was excited. I felt glad to be desperate and miserable enough to think that I might actually seek God with all my heart and soul and mind and strength. And then I concluded by telling the class that church, as most Americans define it, no longer holds any hope for me in my deep desire to experience more of God.

For the first time in fifty-four years of life, forty-six as a Christian, I know an internal sense of freedom to follow the Spirit on whatever path He chooses to take me. I only want Christ and am willing to move in whatever direction the Scriptures mandate and the Spirit leads. I am willing to risk giving up my cultural definition of *church* and try to define it biblically.

When I finished speaking, I felt sheer terror. I guess I did care what people thought, but in a different way. I longed for a certain kind of response. I didn't want to be evaluated, sympathized with, exhorted, or advised. I wanted only to be heard. I yearned for friends to accept me where I was on the journey, and perhaps to let me know what thoughts and ideas my story had stirred within them. After I knew I had been heard, respected, and loved, I felt I would be open to dialogue, including rebuke and correction and exposure of what I didn't want to see. Then, perhaps, I would also receive direction.

I think my fears, although happily not realized that day, were reasonable. We moderns tend to think of our spiritual journey as a God-directed adventure until something goes seriously wrong or until certain problems persist past the time we give God to take them away. Then we think about solving the problems more than about finding God in the midst of them. We focus more on using God to improve our lives than on worshiping Him in any and every circumstance. We think more about pathology—what can be fixed—than about the journey we're on.

As we listen to each other tell our stories, we switch categories from progressing *spiritually* to healing *emotionally* or improving things *circumstantially*. The journey toward knowing God takes a detour. We get off the narrow road of glorifying God and go searching for a rest stop or a refreshment stand or a hospital to make us more comfortable.

Our community feels impotent to us, unable and inadequate to do any real good, the same way you would feel if you told a friend that your tooth hurt. An offer to pray seems less useful than an offer to drive you to the dentist. Consider the kinds of weak sentences we speak to each other when a problem is shared, or even sensed:

- "Maybe you're depressed. Have you considered medication?"

- "I wonder if you've worked through your brother's death. Unresolved grief can generate low-level anger that can really mess you up."

- "As I relate to you, I sense that you're trying to get me to sympathize with you."

- "Your style of relating is self-centered and manipulative."
- "I'll bet that hurts. Your first Christmas since your wife died must be pretty tough."
- "You know, Jesus is really wonderful. Just spend more time in His presence. I know you'll feel better."

An author friend told a group of us about his impending surgery. With some discouragement, he said he would be laid up for several months. "Maybe this will give you a chance to get more writing done," I suggested.

It was a stupid remark. I only wanted to help, but that was the problem. We're a community of fixers. We can't stand to see a problem we can't do something about. We're not *curious about the journey.* We're committed to making things better, to feeling more comfortable, to learning communication skills that will improve our relationships and will make them more satisfying, to relieving pain with empathy.

And we like to *label* each other's problems. Whether the labels are accurate or not, they give us a sense of control. Labels give us the feeling that whatever is wrong is manageable. Somewhere near the center of our approach to community is a failure to see dark valleys for what they are. We don't realize that they do not primarily represent problems to be solved, but are rather *opportunities for spiritual companionship,* for experiencing a kind of relating that is better and different from any we've known before.

Our failure to see things that way is understandable. It's hard to welcome trials as a chance to mature through companionship when no one, including God, shows up. At least no one shows up the way we want them to. When we walk through dark valleys, when our foundations are destroyed, too often we say "flee to God" when we mean "flee to a mountain." When dreams are shattered and life is just terrible, we immediately try to get help. *Nothing matters more!*

That's how we think. It is not our habit to wait on a hidden God to somehow work out a masterful plan to bring glory to Himself. We prefer a different version of waiting. We follow biblical principles or seek counseling to get our kids straightened out, to make our emotions more pleasant, to cause our relationships to be more satisfying. What we really want is a better life.

Many voices in the church, perhaps most of them, speak to that desire: Here's what to do, here's the seminar to attend, here's the counselor to see, here are the principles to follow, here are the rules to keep, here are the biblically exegeted promises to claim. Only a few voices direct us to worship, or call us to a new level of trust. Only a few invite us to experience spiritual conversations in a spiritual community.

Yet you can hear your own heart crying, "It's the *Lord* I want. In the *Lord* I take refuge. I don't want to run to a mountain of relief. Lead me to the Rock that is higher than I, higher than all my troubles, that lifts me into the presence of God. Everything else is secondary!"

That cry from your heart is your longing to be part of a true church, to participate in spiritual community, to engage in spiritual conversations of worship with God and of co-journeying with others. You yearn for a safe place, a community of friends who are hungry for God, who know what it means to sense the Spirit moving within them as they speak with you. You long for brothers and sisters who are intent not on figuring out how to improve your life, but on being with you wherever your journey leads. You want to know and be known in conversations that aren't really about you or anyone else but Christ.

For too long, we've been encouraged by a solution-focused, make-it-work culture to flee to human mountains when life gets tough, when emotional distress and relational tensions and financial struggles threaten to undo us. We've been aiming at an earthbound, this-world version of the blessed life. We've been counseled, medicated, religiously entertained and inspired, exhorted, distracted, and formula-directed long enough. We've lost our focus on spiritual living.

We need a safe place for weary pilgrims. It's time to put political campaigns and ego-driven agendas and building programs and church activities and inspiring services on the back burner. We need to dive into the unmanageable, messy world of relationships, to admit our failure, to identify our tensions, to explore our shortcomings. We need to become the answer to our Lord's prayer, that we become one the way He and the Father are one.

It's time we paid whatever price must be paid to become part of a spiritual community rather than an ecclesiastical organization.

It's time we turned our chairs toward one another and learned how to talk in ways that stir anorexics to eat, multiples to integrate, sexual addicts to indulge nobler appetites, and tired Christians to press on through dark valleys toward green pastures and on to the very throne room of heaven.

It's time to build the church, a community of people who take refuge in God and encourage each other to never flee to another source of help, a community of folks who know the only way to live in this world is to focus on the spiritual life—our life with God and others. It won't be easy, but it will be worth it. Our impact on the world is at stake.

CHAPTER 3

Spiritual Community:
What It Is

I love the church. I do not want to write about the church as a problem,
a source of conflict, a place of controversy, but as the Body of Christ for
us here and now.—Henri Nouwen

The church is a community of people on a journey to God. Wherever
there is supernatural togetherness and Spirit-directed movement,
there is the church—a spiritual community.

One morning when I rose early to pray, I felt the clear leading of God
to invite the members of our family living in Denver to our home for
an evening of worship and prayer. We had been going through some
unusually difficult trials and I sensed a need to gather as a family in the
presence of God. We thought about spiritual warfare, we reflected on a
gospel narrative, we prayed, we shared the Lord's Supper, we cried, and
we sang.

Something wonderful happened during that brief hour. Like manna,
our time spent together was food that nourished us for only a day, but
it stirred a hunger for more. Our hearts met in the life of the Spirit; we
knew what it meant to really be together, supernaturally. None of us were
thoroughly or completely changed—many problems remained, both

within our lives and without—but for a moment, our eyes saw the unseen world and we worshiped. We became more aware of how badly we want to know Jesus.

I cannot describe the thrill of writing about spiritual community as something I've tasted. With conviction, I speak of spiritual community as a gathering of people who experience a kind of togetherness that only the Holy Spirit makes possible, who move in good directions—and *want* to—because the Spirit is at work.

I hesitate to claim that an evening together as a family qualifies as a New Testament church—I don't believe it does—but I have no hesitation insisting that where such community does not exist, there is no church. At its core, the church is a spiritual community journeying together toward God.

In a spiritual community, people reach deep places in each other's hearts that are not often or easily reached. They discover places beneath the awkwardness of *wanting* to embrace and cry and share opinions. They openly express love and reveal fear, even though they *feel* so unaccustomed to that level of intimacy.

When members of a spiritual community reach a sacred place of vulnerability and authenticity, something is released. Something good begins to happen. An appetite for holy things is stirred. For just a moment, the longing to know God becomes intense, stronger than all other passions, worth whatever price must be paid for it. Spiritual togetherness, what I call *connecting,* creates movement: *Togetherness* in Christ encourages *movement* toward Christ.

Bringing these thoughts down to actual conversations is not easy. Right now, as I write these words, it is a little past 6:00 A.M. Later this morning, I will sit with a man whose wife last week announced her intention to divorce him after fourteen years of marriage, and to claim custody of their three small children. He is scared, enraged, and desperate.

We have spoken once already, two days after his wife made known to him her plans. His pain is real. The idea of *visiting* his children is more than he can bear. When I meet with him in a few hours, what will it mean for us to experience spiritual community? What will it mean to be *together,* for the deep places in our redeemed hearts to meet?

And what will it mean to *move*—to move toward Christ? What will it mean for each of us to be stirred to see where life is found when circumstances are hard, to depend on spiritual resources to experience that life, to find within ourselves an overwhelming desire to enjoy the indestructible life of Christ that survives every trial?[1]

Think again upon Henri Nouwen's comment that began chapter 1: "I ponder my experience and I recognize once more that the way for us to be in the world is to focus on the spiritual life." What does that mean? Is it different from what a psychologist, even a Christian one like me, would normally do?

In past years, my mind would have thought about what this man could do to win back his wife, where he had failed, what he could now do differently, and how I might support him if his wife carried through with the divorce. My energy would have been largely directed toward saving the marriage. And I would have asked God to help me, to bless my efforts.

But now I am stirred by a higher vision. It is one that absolutely gives the marriage the best chance it has, but it is a vision that is higher than saving the marriage, a vision that this man can reach and his wife cannot block. He *desires* that his marriage be restored—of course. But his *goal* must be higher.[2]

As I meet with this distressed husband, I want to be in the stream of God's purposes throughout history, purposes that run through this difficult moment but are neither limited to it nor thwarted by it. And I want to invite him to join me. With humbling force, it occurs to me that if anything good happens in our conversation, it will have more to do with who I am than what I can do, more to do with whether I listen to and follow the Spirit than whether I remember my training and use my professional skills. My life in the Spirit matters more than my counseling talent.

Have I prayed? Have I been still enough and honest enough and passionate enough to hear God? Or am I going to meet my friend as a false prophet, one with a message he never heard from God? We will order two cups of coffee, pull up chairs to a small round table in the corner of the coffee shop, and begin talking.

As I anticipate what might happen later this morning, I remember our earlier conversation less than a week ago. I told him then that there is another room in his heart that he has not yet entered, at least not for long, and perhaps has not even known is there. Only as he speaks from that room, I said, will he speak with spiritual energy.

How his wife responds is not under his control—he must not blame or credit himself for what she does—but if he lives in that room and speaks from it, he will know joy, whatever happens. I quoted C. S. Lewis: "Put first things first and second things are thrown in. Put second things first and you lose both first and second things." Winning his wife back and preserving his family are, of course, exceedingly important, to be rightly desired with deep passion. But they are second things, surpassed only by the one thing that is first.

"You were not put on earth to be this woman's husband," I had said. "You were put here to reflect the character of God in the way you live, to pour out His life through yours toward whomever you're with, however they treat you. That's the first thing, to glorify God by worship and trust in every circumstance and by revealing what He's like."

I then added, "The first thing is to find that room, that place in your heart where the Spirit is alive, and to release the spiritual energy He has put there. To abandon yourself to God's purposes. To listen to the Spirit speak through His Word. To think after Him."

The man had listened intently. I was not requiring him to be convinced. I was not determined to help him. Those were *my* second things. For me, the first thing in that conversation was to speak from the upper room in my heart. Other motives were mixed in—they always are—but that's what I most deeply wanted.

Our conversation had borne the marks of spiritual community. We'd met at a level only the Spirit makes possible and we'd both moved another inch on our journey toward God.

He left our first time together saying that this was a different perspective. He had expected me to help him think through the best strategy to soften his wife's heart. During our chat, he'd become aware of how desperately he was *demanding* hope, how *dependent* he felt on any evidence that his wife was backing away from divorce, how *determined* he was, at all costs, to save his marriage.

"You're saying those desires are understandable, even good, but that they can't be in first place. Something stirs as you say that. I feel like I've been invited to that other room. And I want to go."

Now, nearly a week later, we're to meet again. Yesterday's food will not nourish us today. We need another meal. We're a community of two on a journey to God. How can we be together and move?

Between the last sentence you read and the one you're now reading, a half day has elapsed. I'm back at my desk after the second meeting with my friend. Let me give you a few snatches from our conversation.

Friend: "What you said last week stirred me. I could feel something happening in me. But as soon as I got back to the real world of lawyers, settlements, and all the tensions in our house, it all disappeared. It's been an awful week."

Larry: "What stirred last week when we talked?"

It's common for counselors to encourage a recital of painful details, assuming that empathic understanding will encourage further lifting of denial in a nonjudgmental setting. There is a time, of course, when we all need to vent our feelings. But I am more interested in where the Spirit is alive in the midst of life's difficulties than in the details of the troubles.

Friend: "You spoke of me as a hollow man about to become solid. I want that. Even as I say it now, something stirs again."

Larry: "That's your appetite for first things. Any words you speak to your wife out of your hollowness will be manipulative, weak, and demanding. Imagine speaking to her out of solidness. She *may* respond. God *will* be glorified."

I assume the Spirit is always whispering "Abba" to God's children, assuring them that they are safe in His care. And He is continually calling them to become what God saved them to be, solid people, indestructibly alive, hurting perhaps, but consumed with pleasing the

Father. Offering a vision of *what could be* stirs the deep work of God's Spirit.

Friend: "I think I did speak out of solidness once this past week. I told her how I had failed her. But not with the whimpering please-forgive-me-and-come-back kind of attitude I've had. And I wasn't apologizing to set her up for her own apology. I really felt a desire to bless this woman. And for just a moment, she seemed quiet. I think she actually teared up a little. But it's all so confusing. I thought I handled another situation well but she got furious. Then I blew up. It's really bad."

Larry: "That one unconfusing time, I gather, felt good."

Notice how easily my friend loses spiritual focus and returns his attention to his pain and difficult situation. Again, there is a time to share difficult burdens and to just be held, physically or verbally, by someone who cares. But I sensed meaningful energy in his report of speaking once out of solidness. It didn't seem insensitive to his pain to speak to what was deeper in him.

Friend: "Remember what you said about another room in me? I think you were saying that the room I usually live in is the room where I've been hurt, where I've learned to come and try to make my life work. Is that right?"

Larry: "Yes, and it's a big room. Plenty there to keep your attention. My concern is that in this crisis you'll stay in that room and try to clean it up and rearrange the furniture."

Counselors spend wasted time trying to improve what God has abandoned. Sorting things through often has the purpose of understanding what's gone wrong and how to fix it. The Spirit, however, has created another room in our souls, a room that is always clean and well furnished. We need to leave the fascinating room of complex psychological dynamics and find the room where spiritual forces from God are alive.

Friend: "I don't want to do that. I think I found the other room but I only stayed there for a few minutes. How can I learn to stay there longer?"

Larry: "The odds are stacked against you. Your situation is the toughest you've ever faced. You'll feel drawn to focusing on what you can do to make it better. You'll want to dwell on finding out where you're wrong, and where she's wrong. Meanwhile, anger and self-hatred will flood into you like a tidal wave. Unless you want to be in that other room with all your heart, and unless you're willing to literally wait on God to make it real, you won't get there. Your appetite for that new room needs to be nourished."

We then talked about his prayer life, the value of fasting, and a few good books that I've found helpful. He left saying, "I think I'll need help to keep on this path. Can we meet again?"

I think we enjoyed a moment of spiritual community where I was privileged to serve him as a spiritual director more than as a spiritual friend.

In my life and in the lives of so many, these kinds of conversations are unusual. Most often, we engage each other in ways that fall far short of what the Spirit makes possible.

Why? Why is spiritual community so rare? I suspect it has to do with the requirement of brokenness. We'd much rather be impressively intact than broken. But only broken people share spiritual community. That's my key thought in the next chapter.

CHAPTER 4

It Takes
an Armando

There is within me a tendency to play it safe. I want to stay friends with
everyone. I do not like conflict or controversy. Often I think that what
we are living [here Nouwen is referring to his world of quiet friend-
ships] is very similar to what St. Paul and the apostles lived during the
early years of Christianity—intimate celebrations in people's homes,
prayers, conversation and mutual support. Simple but very nurturing.
                            —Henri Nouwen

Only a certain kind of community, what I am calling spiritual community, can cut through our commitment to safety from people
and allow us to enjoy safety with people. Jean Vanier, founder of L'Arche
communities across the world that give disabled people the chance to
discover their true worth and beauty, tells the following story.

In Rome in 1987, the bishops attending a synod concerned with the
role of the laity in the Roman Catholic Church were invited to an unusual
gathering. In Vanier's words,

> . . . the Faith and Light communities of Rome invited all the bish-
> ops to come to a gathering of their communities, made up of people

with intellectual disabilities, their parents and many friends, especially young people. Only a few bishops came. The community of L'Arche in Rome came also, with Armando, an amazing eight year old boy they had welcomed.

Armando cannot walk or talk and is very small for his age. He came to us from an orphanage where he had been abandoned. He no longer wanted to eat because he no longer wanted to live cast off from his mother. He was desperately thin and was dying from lack of food. After a while in our community where he found people who held him, loved him, and wanted him to live, he gradually began to eat again and to develop in a remarkable way.

He still cannot walk or talk or eat by himself, his body is twisted and broken, and he has a severe mental disability, but when you pick him up, his eyes and his whole body quiver with joy and excitement and say, "I love you." He has a deep therapeutic influence on people.

I asked one of the bishops if he wanted to hold Armando in his arms. He did. I watched the two of them together as Armando settled into his arms and started to quiver and smile, his little eyes shining. A half hour later I came to see if the bishop wanted me to take back Armando. "No, no," he replied. I could see that Armando in all his littleness, but with all the power of love in his heart, was touching and changing the heart of that bishop.

Bishops are busy men. They have power and they frequently suffer acts of aggression, so they have to create solid defense mechanisms. But *someone like Armando* [emphasis mine] can penetrate the barriers they—and all of us—create around our hearts. Armando can awaken us to love and call forth the well of living water and of tenderness hidden inside of us.

Armando is not threatening . . . he just says, "I love you. I love being with you."[1]

A spiritual community consists of people who have the integrity to come clean. It is comprised of those who own their shortcomings and failures because they hate them more than they hate the shortcomings and failures of others, who therefore discover that a well of pure water flows beneath their most fetid corruption. *Someone like Armando* is necessary for spiritual community to develop, someone who is loved in his brokenness and therefore pours love out of his very being, with neither hidden nor self-preserving agendas.

Armando's deformities were physical, and therefore impossible to hide. Ours are moral and more easily concealed. Integrity is the first step: We must admit to our community, to a spiritual friend or a spiritual director, who we are at our worst. We must tell our stories to someone without consciously leaving out a chapter.

The response of community comes next. If the response is anything less than unconditional love, our brokenness becomes fragmentation. We present part of who we are to our unsafe community and hide the rest. We disconnect from ourselves and from others. But if someone loves us, as the members of L'Arche loved Armando in both his physical and spiritual brokenness, we discover that something good has survived every trauma, something pure has remained uncontaminated. And we find ourselves pouring it out effortlessly.

It's now four o'clock in the afternoon. Just an hour ago I made a difficult drive to see Rich, a good friend. Two weeks ago I had spoken about him to another friend, disguising Rich's identity but revealing things from our private conversations in order to make a point. Because my second friend did not know Rich and would have had difficulty recognizing him even if he did, I felt I had not violated a confidence.

Early this morning from 7:30 till nearly 9:00, Rich was again discussing sensitive and very personal matters with me, seeking spiritual direction. At one point he said, "You know, what we've been talking about these last few months is pretty touchy. I'm sure glad you don't share this with anyone."

I winced. Up until that moment, I'd had no thought of having breached an ethical standard. Even as I reflected on what I'd said to the second friend, I still didn't view it as a breach.

But I wasn't sure Rich would see it that way. So I smiled and said, "The privilege of sharing with you is too precious to violate in any way."

Within an hour of leaving that conversation, I called Rich and asked to come and talk to him. I made the difficult drive to his office and have just now returned home. I told him what I had done. I explained that my conversation with the other man still did not seem to me a violation of confidentiality, but I confessed that I had lacked the courage to tell him about it when his comment seemed to make it appropriate to do so.

His reply: "I sensed from that point on in our conversation this morning that you were scrambling. In our previous times and up to that point this morning, you always seemed so effortless. I didn't know what happened."

Of course. The living water pouring out of my soul had been blocked by my cowardice. As I stood broken before him, experiencing his grace, the water again flowed. The deepest part of me is not cowardly, it is loving, strong, and good. It is the energy of Christ. Rich felt the impact of who I am as a Christian and I felt the same impact from him. We connected at the level of our common life in Christ. We both felt safe.

Only when the perfume jar is broken in the presence of accepting community is the fragrance released.

Everything in spiritual community is reversed from the world's order. It is our weakness, not our competence, that moves others; our sorrows, not our blessings, that break down the barriers of fear and shame that keep us apart; our admitted failures, not our paraded successes, that bind us together in hope.

A spiritual community, a *church*, is full of broken people who turn their chairs toward each other because they know they cannot make it alone. These broken people journey together with their wounds and worries and washouts visible, but are able to see beyond the brokenness to something alive and good, something whole.

Each of us is wounded. For every one of us, ruthless honesty about what is happening inside of us will lead to brokenness. In a spiritual community, people don't merely talk about woundedness and brokenness. They leave their comfort zones and expose the specifics, not to everyone, but to at least one other person.

It's terrifying to do so. It seems so weak, so unnecessary, so morbid and self-criticizing. Worse, in many eyes, to admit brokenness means to admit a poor relationship with God. We often *hear* that brokenness is the pathway to a deeper relationship with God, but we rarely see it modeled. I sometimes think we want others to believe that we know God by demonstrating how unbroken we are.

But we've all been wounded. We've all failed. Rejection has brought out depths of anger we didn't know were in us. We've sobbed over unkindness and resolved to never let anyone treat us like that again. Our souls have withered under the heat of someone's disdain. Criticism has made us feel worthless, and we've either backed away from involvement or taken life on with defensive arrogance.

We protect our wounds with all the fierceness of a lioness watching over her cubs. And because it is nearly impossible to see who we are as separate from those wounds, we think we are protecting our *selves* when in fact we are preserving our *wounds*.

Beth and I were sharing a meal. She had asked me to provide direction in her spiritual journey. "I think I told you a year ago that when I was twenty-one I had an abortion. I said it quickly and passed over it. But I still feel pretty guilty. I worry that one of my three children will die because I killed my first baby."

What do I say? If he could speak, what would Armando say?

Perhaps a better first question is, What do I feel? I immediately sensed myself pulling back from her, not in disgust but rather in confusion. I wanted to tell her that she was forgiven, that Christ's death had paid for all her sins and there was no judgment left for her.

But she already knew all that. I could feel my desire to "make a point," to pronounce truth and try to persuade her to believe it. Beth could not hear God singing over her with delight, and I had no confidence that *telling* her He was singing would help her hear the song. As we spoke, she was identifying herself as a woman who'd had an abortion, a murderer.

Beth looked nervous. I think she was on her guard, not so much against criticism or judgment; I don't believe she expected that from me. I wondered if she might be more afraid that I would speak to her head and ignore her heart, that I would remind her of what she already knew and expect her somehow to feel the impact of familiar truth simply because I repeated it.

I thought of Armando. I saw myself as Armando, a broken man who could not look down on Beth from higher ground. I couldn't say, "There but for the grace of God go I." That felt condescending. Instead, I whispered to myself, "Who are you that judges another? You need grace every bit as much as Beth."

Then I looked at her. I could see only a scared, broken child who longed for love. My eyes teared up, I felt warmth rising within me and I found the courage to put into words what was deepest in my heart: "Oh Beth, what a horrible load to bear. You must long to be able to just rest and enjoy your children."

The words mattered, but the energy carrying them mattered more. Something poured out of me that spoke to who she was, not to what she had done or even what she feared.

Our longings to be loved at our worst, to enter into a safe relationship of intimacy with Jesus, are far more central to who we are than our failures and fears. But that's difficult to see. We *feel* our guilt and pain more than we *feel* our eager passion to be loved. And we identify ourselves more by what's wrong with us than by what God has made right.

Part of the reason for this is our mad determination to pin labels on each other, our tendency to identify people by their problems. "Did you know he's divorced?" "I just heard she's taking Prozac." "They're the couple with the son in a wheelchair." "Someone told me she's a lesbian." "He's the guy who gets so angry."

We are not our problems. We are not our wounds. We are not our sins. We are persons of radical worth and unrevealed beauty. If we face ourselves fully, we will be broken by what we see, by the selfishness and fear and rage and lust that cover our spiritual beauty like tarnish on silver. But the silver is there. Something brilliant and intact gleams through the stain of our brokenness.

Labeling each other makes the shine of the silver hard to see. It directs attention to the tarnish. Labels encourage us to believe that our problems define us. Of course our problems are never pretty. So we either use them to manipulate people into taking care of us or we hide who we mistakenly think we are.

The passion to play it safe is strong. Vainer said that bishops who suffer acts of aggression committed against them develop thick mechanisms of self-defense, stubborn patterns of self-protection in their relationships. We all do.

The passion to protect ourselves, to keep our wounds out of sight where no one can make them worse, is the strongest passion in our hearts. And it will remain so *until we experience a certain kind of relationship, until we meet the crucified and resurrected Christ, and experience a person like Christ, someone broken yet beautiful, someone like Armando.*

When the bishop held Armando, I presume what he felt most deeply was not the tragedy of a disabled body and a poorly functioning mind but rather the touch of a living soul that poured out pure love. It's that touch that defines connection. It happens only when we have the confidence that ugliness and conflict will not end a relationship, a confidence that grows out of an even stronger confidence that what is deepest within is not brokenness but beauty, the literal beauty of Christ.

It takes someone like Armando to shatter our defenses, to expose our brokenness, and to touch our souls with love. It takes someone like Armando to reveal Christ, to help us see the miracle of the gospel in our hearts, that beneath all the pretense and posturing, beneath the wounds of insecurity and failure, there is divine goodness.

If there is no Armando, if no one is broken enough to enjoy God's love and give it away, our communities never become spiritual. The inevitable conflict that crops up eventually in every relationship will take us in unspiritual directions, into relationships that do not require the Spirit.

In the next chapter, I look at an Armando-less community and discuss what spiritual community is *not*. In unspiritual community, we make certain we are safe *from* people and never enjoy safety *with* people.

CHAPTER 5

Unspiritual
Community

We probably have wondered in our many lonesome moments if there is
one corner in this competitive, demanding world where it is safe to be
released, to expose ourselves to someone else, and to give uncondi-
tionally. It might be very small and hidden. But if this corner exists, it
calls for a search through the complexities of our human relationships
in order to find it.—Henri Nouwen

Without someone like Armando, spiritual community will not develop.
Without a safe community, we will not own our brokenness. We will
not provide others with the safety they need to own theirs. Community will
be a competitive, demanding place where we feel the pressure to demonstrate
that God has done more work in our lives than He has. Or we might turn
in a different direction. We might put a pseudo-brokenness on display and
seize every opportunity to reveal our emotional struggles, demanding, perhaps angrily, perhaps with tears, that others see our pain and take care of us.

In unspiritual community, we tend to either hide our problems or
parade them. In neither case do we give. There is no reflection of the
life of the Trinity.

It is a tragedy to live in unspiritual community. It is an even greater tragedy to live in unspiritual community and be satisfied and to think that it is spiritual. There are many Christians relating in ways that only marginally require the Spirit, and who aspire to nothing more.

I sense, however, as I speak with people across our country, that a growing number can feel their thirst for a distinctly spiritual kind of relating and are finding it difficult to settle for anything less. They are experiencing a vague but undeniable loneliness, an empty awareness that the activities of life only temporarily and partly fill.

Maggie Ross describes the spiritual life as continually beginning to understand that loneliness is really a hunger for God.

> We try to fill up that ghastly hole in the pit of our stomachs that is really in our souls. We try to fill it with food, with power, with sex.... We begin to realize that this hunger will never be satisfied, not in this life. It is the hunger for the Face of God, and the only possible food is prayer.[1]

In the introduction to her book, she defines *solitude* as "... Our fathomless meeting place with God and the wellspring of true relationship.... If we could discover the life of solitude, which lies at the heart of true relationship and is its source, we might find an alternative to devouring one another."[2]

That's what I want. Like you, I want to contribute to spiritual community, to provide my family and friends with a safe place to face their brokenness and find God. Still, after forty-six years of living with the life of Christ within me, I am often unsafe in my response to others. I tend to push my points, to insist that others see what I think they should see.

The wrong sentence can instantly turn out the lights in my soul, and I no longer sense God's presence. Sometimes I don't care if He is there or not. Other times I feel flat or superficially fine. In so many states of being, I can easily devour another, sometimes with pleasant banter: "Hey, nice tie. The two stains are nicely placed," and sometimes with outright attack, "I can't believe you did that! How *could* you?"

I want to do better. I want to be more like Jesus, to be safe and firm and tender and direct. Life is already hard, and I don't want to make anyone's life more difficult. But how do I do it? How do I grow into a person who helps make a community spiritual? I think Maggie Ross is saying that worship is the heart of community, that true relationship with each other—what I call connecting or spiritual community—is not possible without rich and abiding communion with God.

No one knows or is known by another without entering more fully into God's presence. The resources for connecting with each other must be given to us by the Spirit. They can only be nourished by yielding to Him as much as Mary did in order to conceive God's Son.

Spiritual community depends on spiritual resources, and for good reason. Every human relationship, especially where the participants long to experience deep closeness, encounters significant conflict. And there simply is no way through the conflict to true connection without divine power. There is no way through without an energy in the soul that is supplied by God, an energy that is stronger and better than the energy that is already there, fueling the conflict.

Brokenness is the realization that life is too much for us, not just because there is too much pain but also because we're too selfish. Brokenness is realizing He is all we have. Hope is realizing He is all we need. Joy is realizing He is all we want. Dietrich Bonhoeffer wrote: "Our community with one another consists solely in what Christ has done to both of us."[3]

I have spent so much of my life hearing that sort of teaching and thinking of it as true but not immediately necessary to grasp. I now see it differently. I am beginning to understand that the loneliness I have for so long tried to relieve by marrying, by developing friendships, by writing books, by thinking of funny things to say at parties, is really a hunger for God.

When I fail to see that, my loneliness energizes the unbrokenness within me to do whatever I must, and to use whoever is available to fill my soul. And I feel justified in doing so. I *have to*. The pain must be relieved. Surely anyone who could feel my hurt would agree.

Passions *that* ugly and *that* demanding can never be tamed. They cannot be fully hidden, nor can they be weakened by understanding their roots. They can for a time be disguised but they can never be either improved or controlled. Our only hope is that another passion arise within us that is stronger and better. Only the resources of the Spirit are adequate to move us through conflict into true relationship. Only *good* passions supplied by the Spirit can replace the bad ones as the foundation for community and withstand the assault of conflict.

Spiritual communities understand that. They understand that the *presence* of conflict does not define unspiritual community, just as the *absence* of conflict is no proof of spiritual community. The difference between spiritual and unspiritual community is not whether conflict exists, but is rather in our attitude toward it and our approach to handling it. When conflict is seen as an opportunity to draw more fully on spiritual resources, we have the makings of a spiritual community.

Conflict is latent in every human relationship at every moment. It simply awaits a trigger to get it going. Self-occupied passions, the kind that when released generate conflict, are in each of us, simmering beneath our sociable exteriors. They include the tendency to play it safe, to require comfort or attention, to focus on our open wounds more than on our opportunity to give, to demand an immediate fullness that God won't always provide.

In spiritual community, these passions are met by the acceptance of a spiritual friend. This friend sees them, hates them and may rebuke them, is hurt by them and may say so. He or she sees through the ugliness of all those conflict-producing, selfish motives to the sheer goodness that lies beneath, a goodness that has been placed there by God.

When necessary, those bad passions are explored with the wisdom of a spiritual director, not to change them, but to recognize their subtle expressions, to feel their hideous strength, and to celebrate the grace that both forgives and replaces them with something better. That's what happens in *spiritual* community.

Self-occupied passions are not handled that way in unspiritual community. Without finding the divine resources needed to support us through conflict, to free us to forgive and love, we have no adequate response to conflict. We have no way to relax in its presence, no way to avoid hating either ourselves or others, no way to move past grudges and guardedness to compassion and freedom.

We can't deal with conflict any more than a man with a dollar can buy a house. He doesn't have what it takes, and neither do we. We're homeless, fighting ten others for the shelter of the park bench, for the warmth of the one blanket we've found. There *is* conflict. Spouses quarrel, church boards disagree, friends disappoint and betray one another. We have to do something.

In unspiritual community, we hide conflict behind *congeniality.* We re-channel it into *cooperation* on worthy projects where ugly drives become commendable zeal. We soothe the pain we feel because of conflict, using *consolation* to make our pain less pressing. If the conflict is particularly severe, we work through our issues in *counseling.* Or we let *conforming* pressures try to contain our ugliness within renewed efforts to do better.

Instead, we need spiritual friends, *broken* people who will provide safety for us to be broken, *caring* people who want us to live and believe we can live well, *giving* people who pour the life they have received from God into us, people of *vision* who see the Spirit shaping us into the image of Christ. Without them, we settle for so much less.

We settle for an unspiritual community of *congenial relationships, cooperative relationships,* and *consoling relationships,* all counterfeits of spiritual friendship. When these can no longer manage the conflict and handle the ugly passions arising within us, we turn to *counseling relationships* or *conforming relationships* as substitutes for spiritual direction. We do this partly because we can find no one capable to spiritually direct us, and partly because we don't see spiritual direction as our real need.

The situation looks like this:

SPIRITUAL COMMUNITY	UNSPIRITUAL COMMUNITY
The Presence of	The Presence of
CONFLICTED RELATIONSHIPS	CONFLICTED RELATIONSHIPS
met by	handled by
SPIRITUAL FRIENDSHIP	CONGENIAL RELATIONSHIPS
(Care of the Soul)	COOPERATIVE RELATIONSHIPS
	CONSOLING RELATIONSHIPS
and, as needed,	and, as needed,
SPIRITUAL DIRECTION	COUNSELING RELATIONSHIPS
(Cure of the Soul)	or
	CONFORMING RELATIONSHIPS
characterized by	characterized by
DEPENDENCE ON THE SPIRIT	DEPENDENCE ON THE FLESH
(Listening to God through	(Figuring things out through
Word and Spirit)	whatever means are available)

The five kinds of relationships listed beneath "Conflicted Relationships" under "Unspiritual Community" are inadequate responses to inevitable conflict. These responses prove inadequate because they fail to draw on the life of the Spirit present in every Christian. In our culture, they have largely replaced *spiritual friendship* and *spiritual direction,* the relationships that require the resources of the Spirit to function, and are alone able to take us through conflict to spiritual community.

If the church is to develop pockets of spiritual community among its people, a necessary process is to regard conflict in two ways: first, as an opportunity for spiritual friendship to flourish and to do its vital work of soul care. Second, as a reason for spiritual directors to rise up and do their equally vital work of soul cure.

We move away from spiritual community toward unspiritual community when, in response to conflicted relationships, we:

- Hide conflict beneath *congeniality*

- *Cooperate* on a project that lets us continue to honor self-serving agendas

- Seek only *consolation* (relief) when we're in the middle of conflict

- Ask a *counselor* (or therapist) to uncover the roots of our internal conflict in hopes of weakening the passions that cause it

- Double our efforts to *conform* to moral principles of living as our central response to conflict

I am thirsty for spiritual community. In my season on the journey, I have been awakened to my deep joy in worship and my profoundly simple dependence on receiving nourishment from Christ every day through communion with Him in prayer, quietness, meditation, and the Lord's Supper. When spiritual life stirs in the soul, its very nature is to move outward. True life has a mainstream of its own. It longs to share, to meet that same life in another.

Before seminars, I normally pray with my host. Before my most recent seminar, I stayed with my host in his home. We both rose early to pray.

I invited Frank to celebrate the Lord's Supper with me. Our brotherhood never felt stronger. We shared a common life.

I want spiritual community in all its dimensions: prayer, meditation, telling stories, playing, practical helping, supporting in crisis, eating, weeping, laughing, doing ordinary things. What makes it spiritual is the Spirit. No matter what we're doing—sharing ordinary moments or joining together in sublime worship—Jesus Christ is our connection. The energy of Christ is present, passing back and forth between us, creating safety, vision, wisdom, and touching.

But so much of our community time is unspiritual. Perhaps further discussion of unspiritual community and the five kinds of relationships that commonly make it up will help us realize which kind of community we're in. If we find we're in spiritual community, we'll be grateful and eager to love even more. If we realize our relationships are more unspiritual than spiritual, perhaps our thirst for what the Spirit empowers, what Jesus prayed for before He died, "that they may be one," will become strong enough to pay the necessary price.

In the next chapter, I ask what makes unspiritual community unspiritual, and I look more closely at the five kinds of relationships that we sometimes assume are spiritual.

CHAPTER 6

Why Unspiritual Community Is Unspiritual

Our life is full of brokenness—broken relationships, broken promises, broken expectations. How can we live that brokenness without becoming bitter and resentful except by returning again and again to God's faithful presence in our lives?—Henri Nouwen

Community is a place of pain, of the death of ego. In community, we are sacrificing independence and the pseudo-security of being closed up. We can only live this pain if we are certain that for us being in community is our response to a call from God. If we do not have this certitude, then we won't be able to stay in community.—Jean Vanier

One important reason that makes me want to write this book is my growing conviction that all substantial change depends on people experiencing a certain kind of relationship. On a recent trip, a friend drove over to spend an evening with me. A year before, we had enjoyed two days together in the Rocky Mountains. We celebrated another good time together that evening.

I just spoke with him on the phone a few minutes ago. We shared our memories of the more recent time together. I said that during most of the evening I felt effortless as we chatted. I wasn't trying to "help," I didn't work hard, but I quietly depended on the Holy Spirit to stimulate my mind and passions and to share what felt alive.

He had presented a problem that he faced with irritation and irritability. Friends and colleagues often annoy him and he either expresses it or tries to hide it. I remember his words: "I'm sure it has something to do with my father; to this day he's always telling me what to do as if I didn't have a brain in my head. But I've been over that ground before. I don't have much energy to discuss it more."

I offered no interpretations or advice. When we knelt to pray to conclude our evening, I prayed that God would melt his irritation and release the beauty of his patient heart. He told me on the phone a few minutes ago that the words of my prayer have stayed with him, and when he has since felt irritated, he has realized how he *wanted* the anger to soften and his patience to flow. And it's been happening.

I see nothing clever or professional about our interchange, but I do see evidence of the Spirit. I accepted my friend with his irritation. I didn't try to fix his problem through interpretation of underlying dynamics or therapeutic maneuvering. I believed in him and in the power of God's Spirit to release what I knew was already in his heart. Perhaps something came out of me that had power in his life. But there was no pressure, only freedom—the freedom to become who he already is. It's one or the other: pressure or freedom. The two cannot exist together.

For about a hundred years, we have assumed that emotional problems like unreasonable and chronic irritability have an underlying cause that can properly be called a psychological disorder. An *expert* is necessary for *treating* that disorder in much the same way as a trained surgeon knows what to look for in a symptom-filled body and how to remove whatever is diseased. That's what we've thought.

A few people, I among them, are coming to believe something very different, and a fair amount of psychological research is pointing in the direction we're heading.[1] Someone who *relates well* (that, of course, needs definition) is more capable of promoting meaningful change than a trained professional who "does therapy" to a patient as a set of clinical

46

techniques based on well thought out theories of pathology, diagnosis, and treatment.

I believe in that position because I believe that the root of all non-medical human struggle is really a spiritual problem, a disconnection from God that creates a disconnection from oneself and from others. That disconnection consists of a determination to take care of oneself in the face of a disappointing and sometimes assaulting world. We conclude that no one exists who has our best interests at heart. That's *unbelief.*

The resolve to look after oneself (call that *rebellion*) breaks fellowship with God and others and involves a violation of our created nature to be givers (disconnection from self). Worse, it cuts us off from the resources we need to live that are poured into us from God and others, resources that are only poured into us when we are openly and vulnerably and trustingly connected.

We simply do not believe in a God who is so intrinsically good that His commitment to be fully Himself is equivalent to a commitment to be very good to us. When He tells us that He is out for His own glory, and will glorify Himself by making known who He is, we can relax. It's something like a wealthy, generous father declaring his intention to display his true character. We know we're in for a bundle. That is, if we're his heirs.

When Jean Vanier states that community is the place where ego dies, I understand him to mean that *our determination to fully trust no one must die* and an eager willingness to receive what is best from others and to give what is best from within ourselves must take its place. That only happens when people feel loved, *safe* enough to face their dependency, *trusting* enough to enjoy what someone else gives, and *courageous* enough to offer who they truly are to another.

It is a risk. A close friend gave her heart to a man who retreated from her. He ended up leaving her. She is having an enormously difficult time envisioning the possibility of giving her heart again. The temptation to settle for a physical relationship with a man who wants no more than that is a strong one. Does my friend need therapy to work it through? Or would a few spiritual friends help more, people who would accept her with all her confusion, resentment, and terror and quietly believe there is something more in her heart? Perhaps a spiritual director, who could help her look carefully at the powerful demands of the flesh that her rejection has nourished, would also be useful.

I cannot see what a therapist, in the traditional sense of the word, could do. I am having a hard time coming up with a reason to train psychotherapists or counselors. The master's counseling program where I teach has largely shifted to a spiritual formation model of personal change. Our focus is on developing students into spiritual friends and spiritual directors. It may not be too much to say that the reason therapists are busy is that there are so few spiritual friends and spiritual directors.

In *Successful Psychotherapy: A Caring, Loving Relationship*, psychologists C. H. Patterson and Suzanne Hidore admit that psychotherapy is in chaos. Their solution is worth a second look. Professional helping efforts, they suggest, should abandon all hope of identifying specific diagnosable disorders and coming up with specific technical treatment plans. They should instead focus on one simple yet profound idea—that the essence of all successful psychotherapy is love. They go so far as to suggest that their book could well have been titled *Psychotherapy: The Purchase of Love.*[2]

I wholeheartedly agree that when therapists accomplish good results (and many do), it is because they are lovers, in the personal sense of that word, and not experts. But I am disturbed by the idea of *purchasing* love. Purchased love seems like an oxymoron. What can be purchased, or won by any means, is not love. It may be a close counterfeit that, for a time, seems to produce the same effects. But only genuine, unpurchasable love does what needs to be done in the human soul.

Patterson and Hidore quote Jerome Frank, a leading figure in the field of therapy research: ". . . success in therapy depends on the therapist's ability to convey to the patient that he cares, is competent to help, and has no ulterior motive."[3]

But what is this therapeutic relationship intended to cure? The roots of psychological problems and personal battles have to do with one's relationship to God. When it is a bad relationship full of enmity, suspicion, and mistrust, we are left angrily terrified and alone, and therefore desperately determined to keep ourselves safe in an unsafe world. And that is something we cannot do.

If that is what needs therapeutic attention, and if attention that is therapeutic is a relationship of love, wisdom, and integrity, then successful therapy consists of a kind of relationship a spiritual community is uniquely and intentionally gifted to provide. Why, then, do we turn to professionals?

Spiritual people love. They have the wisdom to understand whatever is getting in the way of the Spirit's working, and their motivation is not self-serving. They live to advance the kingdom for God's glory. But spiritual community is rare. That's why we have professionals. And rather than identifying our lack of spiritual community as a huge problem needing attention, we have tried to handle our problems in unspiritual community. In doing so, we offer only congenial, cooperative, consoling, counseling, and conforming relationships to people in conflict.

Beneath everything from eating disorders and dissociative identity disorders, to feelings of irritability and occasional peeks at pornography, is a proud spirit of independence that is our foolish response to the terror of being alone. It is a bad spirit that only a good spirit can replace. When that is more clearly understood, perhaps our desire will be rekindled to see the word *church* defined as "spiritual community."

Perhaps we'll search through human complexity to find a corner of safe community and will return again and again to God's faithful presence in our lives. Perhaps, through all the squabbling and pain, we'll hear God's call to stay in community until we become spiritual friends and directors.

Look with me now at *conflicted community*, what we must all deal with, and then more briefly at the five kinds of relationships that unspiritual community offers in response.

Conflicted Community

My intention in discussing conflict is to make only one point: Conflict is a problem only spiritual community can handle. Listen first to the apostle James pinpoint his inspired understanding of why it exists.

What causes fights and quarrels among you? Don't they come from your desires that battle within you? You want something but don't get it. You kill and covet, but you cannot have what you want. (James 4:1–2 NIV)

Conflicts arise when people have opposing agendas, competing agendas where something deeply personal is at stake.

I have never easily believed in my ability to do something well. In order to relax even somewhat before, during, and after a talk, I must be thoroughly convinced that whatever I have to say was given to me by the Spirit. When I lose at chess (a rather frequent occurrence), a thought darts through my mind: *This is a thinking person's sport. Your mind isn't too sharp.* From the soil of fear, a deeply personal agenda develops, a demand that I be affirmed. The framework for conflict is in place.

I don't really know where that tendency came from. My parents love me, are proud of me, and have always supported whatever I wanted to do. Still, I've not been a confident person. Maybe the roots lie deeper than my background. I think they do. When we go back into our personal histories to discuss the reason for our struggles, we usually don't go back far enough. We need to travel all the way back to conception.

All of us enter life with a severe handicap: We trust no one, and our deepest inclination is to seize from life what we need while protecting ourselves from its disappointments and threats. That strikes me as a rather substantial handicap if we are designed to be in true community. Sociologist Ashley Montagu sees it differently:

> My own interpretation of the evidence leads me to the conclusion that man is born good and is organized in such a manner from birth as to need to grow and develop his potentialities for goodness.... All the available evidence gathered by competent investigators indicates that man is born without a trace of aggressiveness.[4]

If we are the product of evolutionary chance and can therefore justify a survival-of-the-fittest brand of individualism, then I suppose a need to develop our potential could be seen as adaptive. But if a Trinity of

Persons created us to enjoy spiritual community, then self-development as a primary drive is indeed aggressive. It represents a determination to use you for my well-being because that is of higher value to me than your well-being. In a fundamentally relational world, it is difficult to see how that can be understood as something other than selfishness.

Psychologist Charlotte Buhler found that there is "evidence of a primary orientation toward 'reality' into which the baby moves with a positive anticipation of good things to be found. Only when this reality appears to be hurtful or overwhelming does the reaction become one of withdrawal and defense."[5]

But the reality is good because it satisfies the baby. And that's our natural definition of goodness—something that makes us feel immediately good. When reality doesn't satisfy, the passion to protect oneself against the world rather than give oneself to the world—a passion that was lying dormant—is aroused. This passion seems to me to be a serious impediment to good, Trinitarian-style relating.

And Abraham Maslow, well known for his hierarchy of needs model, "declares that hate, jealousy, hostility, and so on are acquired."[6] Patterson and Hidore, after quoting these recognized authorities, conclude that "there is no instinct of aggression that seeks expression or discharge without provocation or without regard to circumstance."[7]

A growing number of psychologists, particularly those associated with the third stream of psychology (the human potential movement, as opposed to first stream psychoanalysis and second stream behaviorism) believe that the central motivating drive in human nature is self-actualization. This is defined as the basic tendency toward the preservation and enhancement of the self.

I think that's true. I think we are naturally determined to protect and develop our selves. But I think it's a problem. These psychologists believe it's good. I think it's bad.

If God created us and if He is good, then why would our core passion not be to celebrate Him, imitate Him, get to know Him, and reveal Him by the way we relate as the most wonderful loving Person in all the world? Why are we so concerned with looking after ourselves? If God exists and is who He claims to be, then our primary drive toward self-actualization is evidence that something has gone wrong with human nature. It is not something to honor. It is something to worry about.

A biblical theology of the Fall agrees that people are committed to their own self-actualization, to seeking their own security and significance. But that fact is a terrible problem. In a Trinitarian universe, where final reality is other-centered relationship, the priority drive toward self-actualization is selfish and out of step with the way things are supposed to be.

When I enter a group, I am keenly aware of how people react to me. I have a hard time believing that I am wanted and loved. If someone seems to like me, I am drawn to that person. If I am criticized or neglected, something inside crumbles, and then is transformed into rage and defensiveness.

No doubt these tendencies could be traced to a variety of childhood embarrassments, like stuttering and feeling socially out of it as a Christian among mostly secular classmates who didn't invite me to their parties. But such experiences only *shaped* my self-concern; they did not *create* it. Analysis of the shaping influences from my earlier life might help me shift my self-concern to more effective expressions, and might help cure my "social anxiety." But no analysis has the power to shift self-concern to other-concern. That requires stronger help from another source. It requires the gift of a new nature.

We all carry with us a few deep pockets of hurt, vivid memories of painful moments when our self-worth hit the skids. Those moments taught us to define "life" as whatever experiences provided us with a sense of self-worth. "Death" is whatever took it away. With this knowledge of life and death, good and evil, we live for ourselves. And community is ruined.

When I was in eighth grade, I caught the basketball from the opening jump and raced to the wrong end of the court to score a basket. I felt humiliated. That was death. Life, I decided, was to never make a mistake, to do well and be applauded. But could I do it? I had to continually be on guard to avoid foolish mistakes; I had to work really hard to do things well.

Last week I engaged a student in my counseling class about a problem she was experiencing. Sixty students watched. I remember thinking of something that seemed perceptive and wise. I immediately said it. Why? To bless the student? No, to score two points in the right basket. I enjoyed the murmurs of the class. "How did he know to do that? He's good!"

Two things happened because of what I did. First, I set myself up for conflict. The one student who later challenged my direction annoyed me. Second, the energy coming out of me, like a boomerang, came right back into me. Even though my comment was perceptive, nothing of love poured out of me into her. My comment had no power to change her life. That wasn't its intent.

As long as our core passion is self-actualization, the satisfaction of our needs and the realization of our potential and insulation against further hurt, conflict will lie in waiting. When our agendas directly compete with someone else's self-occupied agendas, conflict will erupt. What do we do? In the modern world, we depend on one of five kinds of relationship to handle the conflict, none of which belong to spiritual community.

Congenial Relationships

It's good to enjoy whatever is enjoyable about someone else. That's legitimate congeniality. It's not good to keep ourselves at a distance from another to avoid a clash of opposing agendas, to enjoy another person by refusing to draw close enough to risk conflict. That is defensive civility. It is illegitimate congeniality.

I don't want to be heard to suggest that we should invite conflict by fully speaking our mind. We can never freely be all that we are till heaven. I am suggesting that we recognize impending conflict and realize its source may be in us. We may be honoring our tendency to preserve and enhance ourselves and be missing the opportunity to express what is deeper within us as spiritual people.

Congeniality provides no cure for conflict. It simply hides it.

Cooperative Relationships

Sometimes we move past congeniality into cooperation. We work together on projects that let us channel our self-serving agendas into doing apparent good.

I am familiar with an elder board that sees its core mission as managing the business of the church. The elders speak of their responsibilities to shepherd the flock, but they devote little time to that mission. Managing church business (an important task) certainly brings out competing ideas about how it best should be done, but in the case of this board, the agendas are rarely deeply personal. Involving themselves in people's lives as shepherds, I suspect, would arouse agendas where more was at stake. For example, working with a couple might make the elders look at the conflict in their own marriages. Certainly, if they do their work well, it will.

The pursuit of business keeps these elders safe while still doing "good" things. Conflict, at least the kind that requires abundant grace to move through, is thus avoided.

Consoling Relationships

C. S. Lewis once told a graduating class at Cambridge University that no greater temptation would face them than the urge to create an inner ring of community that was special because it excluded others.

When we find ourselves at odds with Dick, it is comforting to find someone else who doesn't particularly like Dick. Now we have an inner ring. It's a community of two people who exclude Dick. Something deep within us feels justified in our disdain for Dick and comforted in the fellowship of someone who feels the same way. We experience a sense of belonging *here* by not belonging *there*, and by spending time with people who don't belong there either.

A more obvious form of consoling relationship develops when a friend takes on the job of helping us feel better about ourselves. That becomes his or her greatest priority. This bears little resemblance to our Lord's response to Peter. He called him "Satan" and told Peter to get behind him.

Pastors sometimes say what the itching ears of their congregations want to hear. Prostitutes do whatever their clients desire. There really isn't much difference. In each, consolation is the point.

Counseling Relationships

For years, I worked hard as a counselor, trying to figure people out. Why has this teenage girl stopped eating? What is the relationship of early abuse to a current struggle with multiple personalities? Could my client's sexual addiction have grown out of a poor relationship with his father that made him feel inadequate to relate to his wife in a sexually mature way? And what can I do about it? What's the most effective treatment I can render as a paid professional?

Those are the questions most counselors ask. They may be the wrong ones. I think they are.

Analyzing underlying causes and working with the psychological dynamics created by dysfunctional backgrounds are efforts to release self-serving tendencies in a more adaptive manner. In biblical language, it amounts to little more than rearranging or socializing the flesh. Counselors who work with the natural energy within a person to promote healthier living are failing to take advantage of the supernatural energy the Spirit has created in their souls.

Whatever improvement develops is not empowered by the Spirit. It represents no movement toward Christ and spiritual maturity, and it fails to equip the person to contribute to spiritual community.

Conforming Relationships

With so many others, I have felt strong pressure to measure up to certain standards. Of course I understand that my perfection is not required for salvation—it is Christ's perfection that wins me my place in heaven. But still I often feel (and rightly so) that I should be doing better. I know justification is a gift, but sanctification seems like something earned. That's how many Christians see it.

Conforming relationships build on that assumption. They present the opportunity to apply biblical principles to our lives in order to help us try harder to do better. Biblical counseling is sometimes thought of as nothing more than hearing a person's story, identifying where biblical morality is violated, and exhorting the transgressor to conform his behavior to biblical standards.

Relationship, as I am describing it, has little part in the process. Hold the counselee accountable, pray with him, encourage the practice of spiritual disciplines, but don't concern yourself with your own motives as you counsel, or with whether your client feels safe from judgment that is past, and loved enough to hear God singing. Conformity—"do it right"—is the key. Releasing spiritual passions is not highly valued.

My burden is to see spiritual communities develop, where spiritual friends and spiritual directors *connect* with people. I long to see communities where people feel *safe* enough to be broken. Where a *vision* of what the Spirit wants to do in people's lives sustains them, even when they are far from it. Where *wisdom* from God sees what the Spirit is right now doing and what is getting in His way. Where the literal life of Christ pours out of one to energize that life in another, offering His divine *touch*.

What I have in mind are connecting relationships as a response to conflict, not congenial, cooperative, consoling, counseling, or conforming relationships. I've tasted this kind of community. The taste is sweet.

But we must heed Bonhoeffer's warning not to love the *idea* of community, but to love our brothers and sisters. And we will love each other well if we understand both our struggles, what Jesus Christ has done *for* us and *in* us, and wants yet to do on our behalf.

Part II attempts to provide that understanding. I think we will come to see that we must return to God's faithful presence again and again if we are to participate in what the Spirit is up to in each of our lives. And I hope we will also see that God has called us to spiritual community, with Him and with His people. It isn't an option, it is a command. But far more than that, it's the greatest privilege and joy we've been offered.

PART II

A Way of Understanding Our Struggles

CHAPTER 7

Two
Rooms

The Christian life is different: harder, and easier. Christ says,
"Give me all. I don't want so much of your time and so much of your
money and so much of your work. I want You. I have not come to torment your natural self, but to kill it. No half-measures are
any good. I don't want to cut off a branch here and a branch there,
I want to have the whole tree down. Hand over the whole natural self,
all the desires which you think innocent as well as the ones
you think wicked—the whole outfit. I will give you a new
self instead. In fact, I will give you Myself; my own will shall
become yours."—C. S. Lewis

The seminar was fifteen minutes from beginning. We had been worshiping God in music for three quarters of an hour. It was now 7:45
on a Friday evening, and I would start speaking at 8:00.

I stopped singing to listen to something rising within me. It was a
prayer.

"Lord," I heard myself say, "if this message about connecting and a
new level of community is from You, I must know. If I've made it up to

give myself something to think and talk about as I grow older, I want to scrap it.

"But if it is really from You, I want to know it with a certainty I cannot deny. And . . ."—I hesitated; the next thought forming in my mind seemed pushy—"I'd like to know this weekend."

I prayed the prayer inaudibly. No one heard me but God.

Nearly everyone else in that large auditorium was standing to worship. I knew that I would be on my feet for the next two hours, so I was sitting. The chair to my immediate right on the front row was empty.

A few moments after I finished my prayer, a man I didn't know slid onto it.

"May I have a word with you?" he asked.

I nodded quizzically, with a slight edge to my nod. After all, I was praying and about to address a large group for two hours. I thought he was a bit rude.

He told me his name, then said, "I am on the pastoral staff of this church. We've never met, but since the day we invited you to our church, the Lord has laid you on my heart. I feel strongly impressed to say something to you. I intended to wait till after the seminar but I feel I must tell you now. I'll only be a minute."

I nodded again, this time with no edge.

"I sense that you want confirmation from God that your new direction in ministry is from Him, and that you want it this weekend. I believe God has called you to what you're doing and He wants me to tell you that this weekend you'll know."

A few more words and he slipped away.

I'm not telling you that to persuade you of my call from God. I record the incident, rather, to say that the man's words spoke to a part of my heart that few words reach. I've since wondered how often the words I say come out of those largely unused depths of who I am.

I have no doubt that the man's words to me emerged from the new self Christ had given to him, and that's why they reached the new self within me. We met at the deepest level of our being, where the Spirit of Christ has chosen to live.

What did Jesus mean when He announced that He and His Father would *make their home* in us (John 14:23)? Picture your soul as a dwelling place with two rooms.

One of the rooms is self-furnished. You have spent your life buying sofas, arranging lamps, and hanging pictures on the wall. It's a comfortable room. It suits your taste. Your resources were limited, but you did what you could. It is now a place where you can relax and feel at home; not fully of course, but it does offer the comfort of familiarity and the pride of ownership. The cushions on the sofa are dented by your contours, you can find the light switch without looking, and you generally remember where you left the remote control for the television.

But when you stretch out and rest in this room, *especially* then, you feel strangely alone. You have this sense that there is another room that fits you better, one you had no hand in furnishing, a place where you might feel less comfortable for a time, but would still very much want to be.

You try to dismiss the thought, to count the blessings where you are: your family and friends, your church, your job and leisure activities, your ministry. But thoughts of the other room keep intruding. It holds an eerie fascination, like the attic in your grandfather's big old house did when you were little, even before you found it and crawled inside.

More than once you've risen from your familiar sofa and gone looking for this other room. But it's hard to find. You remember the first time your hand rested on the knob of the door that led into it. You felt weak. Turning the knob seemed like lifting a boulder. And you were afraid, although you couldn't be certain of what felt so frightening. It was easier to return to *your* room where the door always stands open.

Call the first one the *Lower Room* and the second the *Upper Room*. But keep in mind that the spatial implications of those labels are misleading. The strange room, the *Upper Room*, is really in the center; it is more "you" than the familiar one, which lies close to the center and only seems to define who you are. It really doesn't. That room is your *lower* nature, the *Lower Room*.

The *Upper Room* is the new self Christ gives to any who ask, a higher, better nature that draws its energy from Christ Himself. The idea of two natures can be overdone. We can come to see ourselves as a spectator at a wrestling match, watching the good guy take on the bad, and that's not what I intend. I have in mind what Madame Guyon spoke about in her book, *Experiencing the Depths of Christ*. She invited us to come to a better place to live, a place we could find within ourselves if we learned what it meant to *behold the Lord*.

> The way to do this is really quite simple. First, read a passage of Scripture. Once you sense the Lord's presence, . . . the Scripture has served its purpose; it has quieted your mind; it has brought you to Him.[1]

She later quotes Augustine who once lamented that "he had lost much time in the beginning of his Christian experience by trying to find the Lord outwardly rather than by turning inwardly."[2]

The idea of two rooms is not new. For centuries, spiritual directors in the church (like Augustine and Teresa of Avila) have been telling us of another place to be, an abiding in Christ that is like entering another room, an upper room, the one the Lord built in our souls where He waits ready to meet us. Paul's words "Christ in you" are not merely a metaphor. "Christ in you" is not a lovely thought meant to stir warm feelings. It is a reality, a fact, a firm, unembellished truth. Of course Jesus Christ's literal human body is not in us. But His Spirit is.

One of my wife's good friends recently died, and Rachael attended the funeral. Now the woman's devoted husband will go to bed alone. He will sit at the kitchen table alone. Perhaps he will still sense his wife's presence with him, but it will never be the same as before. She is not there.

But when Jesus returned to heaven, He left more than a memory, more than a lingering sense of someone who is now gone. He told us it would be better for us if He left, because then His Spirit—the personal energy and life that coursed through His human being during the days of His life on earth—would enter into us. And He, the Spirit of Christ, an actual person, would not only come into us, but He would become part of us—the deepest, truest part of who we are.

Now there are two rooms inside us, the one we built where our natural self thrives, and the one the Spirit built where our natural self suffocates and our new self flourishes. Let me describe what I mean by our natural self.

We are persons, bearers of God's image, who long to be in relationship, to both give and receive. That reality is neither moral nor immoral, it just is, like the fact that water is wet and dust is dry.

The moral issue enters the picture when we see that we are stubborn independents, determined to manage our own lives and look after our own needs. Psychologists, as we discussed earlier, call this the drive to self-actualize, a commitment they think is honorable, a yearning to preserve and enhance one's own well-being.

The Bible calls it the *flesh* and says it must die.

So we are fleshly image bearers who have entered the world, who feel its joys and sorrows. We try to figure out the safest and best way to get along in a world of white beaches and dirty ghettos, of abundant buffets and empty refrigerators, of anniversary celebrations and divorce proceedings, of a daughter's graduation from medical school and a son's forced admission into a drug abuse treatment facility.

We hurt, we laugh, we worry. We sing, we scream, and all the while we are scrambling to somehow survive with whatever happiness we can find.

There's one more element in this picture. We have a conscience. We disfigure it, trample on it, ignore it, modernize it, and violate it, but still we think some things are right and some things are wrong. We may shrug our shoulders when a president we'll never meet has an affair, but it's a different story when it's *our* spouse who cheats. We can't eliminate the word *wrong* from our vocabulary.

And the word always comes back to judge us. Group therapist Irving Yalom plays the Top Secret game with people in his groups. He asks them to write out the single thing about themselves they are *least* inclined to share and to then return the paper unsigned. The most frequent top secret is the admission "I feel utterly worthless. No one would want me if they knew me." That didn't surprise me. The number two response did: "I don't love anyone the way I should."

Where did the word *should* come from? Even in our postmodern world, we cannot erase the law of God that is written on our hearts. We were designed to love just as surely as geese were made to honk and cows to moo. The idea of *should* or *ought* is in us. We should honor promises, and certainly folks who promise *us* something should keep their word. We should respect other people's property. No one ought to hop in a car that's not theirs and drive off.

These are the furnishings in the Lower Room: (1) We long for good relationships; (2) we look after our own needs; (3) the world both frustrates and satisfies us, sometimes more one than the other; we learn what we like about the world and go after it; and (4) we are aware of a moral code that tells us what we should or should not do in our pursuit of happiness.

That is life in the first room. God isn't there—at least, He isn't recognized or taken into account. But that's where most of us live.

There is a second room, another place, another way to live. In every human heart there is the sense of something more. The primitives in Plato's cave thought they were living in the real world when they had never seen a bird, never smelled a flower, never watched a sunset. When they were told they were in a cave, that a bright world existed outside, they panicked and killed the messenger. They knew there was something more but they were afraid of it.

C. S. Lewis once said that if we discover desires within us that nothing in this world can satisfy, we really should wonder if we were designed for another world. And those desires are there—God has set eternity in our hearts. Cars and sex and power and achievement are not big enough to fill the space. We long to be caught up in things bigger than living in the Lower Room can ever provide.

In people not yet connected to Christ, the better room is there but it's dark. (I am speaking of the eternal soul in every person.) The electricity has not yet been hooked up. And there are no furnishings. The door to this Upper Room is locked—it can be opened only from the inside. All that's inside is a dead soul. What was meant to be a living room has become a cemetery.

But when the Spirit resurrects the soul and infuses it with new life, the room sparkles with light. The fire in the fireplace roars with crackling heat, the icy heart thaws, and the thrill of life fills the room.

People long for relationship. In the Upper Room, it already exists. No one *demands* relationship in this room. They already have it, and they know that one day they will fully and forever enjoy its pleasures. And people in the Upper Room aren't obsessed with figuring life out. They prefer to live life rather than to analyze it. They have no sense that something fragile within them needs protection and no compelling urge to find themselves. They have already been found. With the pantry full, their strongest desire is to set another place at the table and invite someone else in to enjoy the feast.

The world outside the Upper Room still has white beaches and dirty ghettos. But from the Upper Room they seem like shadows. New cars and cancer surgery and beautiful grandchildren and terrible rejection are still present, but now they are all second things. First things are all in the Upper Room.

When someone leaves the Upper Room, the shadows gain substance, second things become first, and the person who was solid as long as he stayed in that room now becomes a ghost. Leaving the Upper Room always means entering the Lower Room, trying once again to manage the difficulties of life, and every day becoming less and less substantial—more of a ghost than a solid person.

As I describe these two rooms, I am aware of how often I live in the lower one and of how many influences try to keep me there. Sermons that tell us how to make life work and how to discover the fulfillment we want by doing this or that speak to the wrong room. And I'm foolish enough to enjoy them. The best-selling books in America today are self-help books. *You* can do it; you *can* do it! Whether the message comes from self-help gurus or pastors, most of us eat it up.

More people live in the Lower Room than in the Upper Room. The message that Lower Room dwellers want to hear is therefore more marketable. It sells. And people in the Lower Room sometimes live there quite happily for a long time. They see no value in brokenness and radical trust because their own resources are keeping life together quite well.

So many of us enjoy congenial friendships. We cooperate with like-minded folks to raise money for good causes and bring meals to the sick. We depend on a few reliable sources of comfort when things get rough, maybe a beer and a football game or a sexy movie or a nice church service. If things get too confusing and painful, there is always a counselor to give us perspective. And if our conscience points out areas of irresponsibility and failure, we might ask a few moral friends to help us conform to better standards.

For most people, that's life. It's what I earlier called unspiritual community. It seems to work. We're comfortable there and have no strong desire to leave. But something is happening in our culture. The end of modernity, a resurgence of interest in spirituality, and a greater vulnerability about our disillusionment and disappointment with life have made us seriously wonder if there is another room.

In the comment that introduced chapter 5, Henri Nouwen suggested that in our lonesome moments we have all probably wondered if there is one corner in this competitive world where it is safe to relax, to be known, and to give. If there is, if another room exists, then it is worth the search through all the complexities and struggles of human community to find it. That was Nouwen's thought. Honest people agree.

People are becoming aware that there must be another room, a safe corner, a place to deeply relax and know peace. We are admitting that true life and true community and true joy are not available in the room that for so long we have called home.

Over coffee two days ago, my friend Charlie put it this way: "I'm tired of the noise. I can't hear my own heart beating. I just flew back into town. It struck me that airports, with their rows of attached seats and important people and garbled announcements that for one merciful moment shut off the Muzak, are really noisy. But my whole life is like that. I've got to find a quiet place." Charlie is searching for the Upper Room. Our freneticism is really our thirst for heaven's stillness, just as our loneliness is our hunger for God. We want to be in a different room.

When the disciples asked Jesus where He wanted them to prepare the Passover meal, He said, "As you enter the city, a man carrying a jar of water will meet you. Follow him to the house that he enters, and say to the owner of the house, 'The Teacher asks: Where is the guest room, where I may eat the Passover with my disciples?' He will show you a large upper room, all furnished. Make preparations there" (Luke 22:10–12 NIV).

A man carrying water would be noticed. In the culture of Jesus' day, that was a woman's job. Today, someone carrying water stands out among the thousands who have only cotton candy. Thirsty people follow that person.

It's a good picture of the Holy Spirit leading us into the place where we will meet Jesus. It's a good picture, too, of those the Spirit fills, of spiritual friends and spiritual directors who can take us to that Upper Room. I have two rooms in my heart. The man at the seminar carried water and led me to the Upper Room. He spoke to it and I knew it was there.

If we hear only words that are spoken to the Lower Room and if we spend our time there, we will live like citizens of that room. We will:

- Lack power to control sexual appetites
- Be open to connection with evil spirits
- Depend for happiness on people, places, and things other than God and, when they fail to come through for us, we will be devastated
- Find it impossible to get along at intimate levels due to jealousy, tensions, fits of rage, and a spirit of inner-ring exclusion
- Yield to our impulses to feel good now, regardless of the long-range outcome

But if we listen to spiritual friends and spiritual directors who lead us to the Upper Room and speak to us there, and if we stay in that room long enough to share a meal with Jesus, we will:

- Find ourselves wanting to bless people more than use them
- Discover an unshakable joy that survives the most crushing disappointments
- notice a patient and kind gentleness nudging aside our irritation with people
- Experience ourselves as solid and whole in the presence of those who used to intimidate us[3]

Rachael and I spent last weekend with good friends. As we said good-bye, Sheila said, "I wish someone could make me strong."

I know Sheila well. Her Lower Room is full of hard memories from an alcoholic father and clinging mother. To preserve the shreds of her self-esteem, she has learned to be compliant. Sometimes her resentment over being so badly dishonored shows itself in efforts to control, to be noticed and taken seriously.

I've prayed for Sheila. And if I had hours with her, I would not spend much time exploring her Lower Room. I would spend no time trying to rearrange it through insight and advice. For her to become strong, she doesn't need to be psychologically fixed. She needs to change rooms.

I wrote her a letter yesterday. I haven't mailed it yet, and I really don't know if it will speak to her or not. I hope it will. It may encourage movement on a long journey. This is an excerpt from that letter, edited a bit to preserve confidentiality.

> Only one regret from our visit. I heard your desire to be made strong. I wish Rachael and I had hours to think, talk, pray, and celebrate your life together with Gary. Warmth flows out of you toward Rachael and me. We feel it. And I believe it's coming from a place in you that's already strong and good. You just haven't learned yet to rest in that place.
>
> One way to connect with your new heart and all the strength that is there waiting to develop and be enjoyed might be to ask the Spirit, on a daily basis, to reveal your new heart to you, and to remove whatever keeps you from releasing what's there. Ask Him to help you live in the room within you that He's already created, a room full of the life you so badly want.
>
> Ask Him once a day in a sort of liturgical style—on your knees in the same place every day for maybe five minutes—to let His strength in you spring up into your awareness. Then write in a notebook whatever comes to mind as you meditate on a Scripture passage before you face the day.
>
> I read one writer who said—and I agree—that in communion with God you see and hear whatever you need in order to quietly

pour out your truest self into others. Your family is blessed by God's provision of you. There really should be a dinner to celebrate the reality of Christ in you. That's an event I want to emcee.

I have spent most of my professional life trying to understand why the furniture has been so poorly arranged in people's Lower Rooms. I want to spend the rest of my community life enjoying the Spirit's arrangement of furniture in people's Upper Rooms. But to change rooms, to hear the Spirit speak through His Word to us, to enjoy communion with Christ and sense the Father's presence, and then to speak from that room into the reality of our difficult lives, two things need to happen.

One (and the order is not always the same), with the help of spiritual community and through meditation on God's Word and passionate prayer, we need to see our Lower Room for what it is:

- An effort to manage life without God
- A priority determination to preserve and enhance our selves
- A furious hatred of God that fuels a proud, noble-feeling spirit of independence
- A resolute dependence on resources that we use to keep ourselves together and to find happiness

We need to see how we do that, especially in our relationships, so we can present it to God for execution.

Two, we need to join a church, to become part of a community of people on a journey to God. We must spend time with spiritual friends to know them and be known by them and to occasionally ask a seasoned saint to direct us spiritually. And we must learn to be a spiritual friend, and perhaps a spiritual director, to a few others.

As I write these words, I feel suddenly overwhelmed by what could happen in our lives if we actually did those two things. It would take time, but it would be staggering.

In the next two chapters, I further describe the Lower Room. I hope to help us see it for what it is. I long for us to feel an excitement, a desperate desire to find a man carrying water who can lead us to our Upper Room.

I am aware that the Lower Room is an ugly place full of demons and darkness. Looking at it can be discouraging. Before I ask you to explore it with me, let me conclude this chapter with a description of one woman's Upper Room.

Cheryl is a deeply spiritual woman, a developing mystic. Like the rest of us, she struggles, sometimes badly, but she often spots the man carrying water and finds her way to an Upper Room furnished with her in mind. I asked her to describe that room. Here's what she said:

Cheryl's Room

This room—it is so soft. Everything is rounded and the shadows are barely baby blue. It is white, warm, and clean. It is a place to be born into.

I see myself there, but what I am wearing is hard to imagine. Yet I would be clothed, clothed in nothing that draws attention away from or contrasts with the room. Rather, I am blended with the room wearing something so grand you will barely notice me at all.

I so thoroughly enjoy the room that my essence cannot be separated from it. And yet I am there, and it is there and the Light is there. Without the Light there is nothing.

And yes, I desire visitors and welcome them into my room. Indeed, one of its greatest pleasures is to have a guest come in to feel the softness and warmth of it, to sit and to be, to watch as the sheer folds lift and part, to let purity in through the most beautiful window you've seen.

Let freshness caress you and be ye cleaned. It is softly quiet; let it in and drift with it. Your eyes will see delicious. You will know rest and peace.

You will know the truth of the Light, the strength of what holds this room and you will know trusting. You will be tempted to drink me up, but I am not the source or the substance. The substance comes from the Lover of my soul. We meet here, and you are welcome.

Now, with the fragrance and vision of this room lingering, let's look at the other one.

CHAPTER 8

There Is a
Lower Room

*Our greatness and wretchedness are so evident that the true religion
must necessarily teach us that there is in us some great principle of
greatness and some great principle of wretchedness.*—Blaise Pascal

I have had moments when I wondered if my faith would survive. A few months ago, in the middle of excruciating trials that prayer didn't seem to touch, I shouted at the top of my lungs, "God, I know You're good. I *believe* that. But I'm having a hard time knowing what You're good for now, right now, when things are terrible."

Last night, a close friend described what it felt like to wheel his incoherently mumbling father into the nursing home where he had just been admitted, down the urine-smelling hallway to the small room that was now his home. As my friend poured out his sorrow, something deep within me screamed, "God where are You? Do something miraculous. You have the power! *Use it!*"

Not every desperately poor person receives a surprise cash influx in the nick of time—sometimes all that comes in the mail is another bill. Not every person in physical pain finds relief. Not every person who grieves finds her tears wiped away.

Only one time in my life did chucking the faith seem not only possible, but imminent and almost necessary. I remember what, at least from my perspective, kept me anchored. Three people came to mind; their faces and their lives flooded my awareness. If I were to deny the faith with even a scrap of integrity, I knew I would have to go to each of these people and pronounce them deceived.

I couldn't do it.

I've never seen the Red Sea divide or the sun stand still or a man rise out of his coffin. But I have seen the forces of wretchedness overcome in substantial measure by the forces of greatness. I *know* I've seen it in these three people.

Each of them is *solid*. That's the best word. They have suffered and felt it deeply. They have known dishonor and heartbreak, exposing their clay feet. I know two of them well enough to see the lingering traces of wretchedness.

But a life radiates from them that seems indestructible and uncorrupted, solid rather than ghostlike. It's a life that draws me. I like it. I want it. And I cannot explain its existence apart from the gospel of Jesus Christ. I'm still a believer, in large measure, thanks to them. True religion has taught me the "great principle of greatness" through the witness of these three lives.

Unless we have some understanding, however, of the "great principle of wretchedness" and can see it in ourselves, we will not be impressed by its opposite. The lives of folks like the three I've mentioned will not seem so miraculous. And we'll not seek after greatness as a poor man would seek gold. We'll not desire it above all else, nor chase after its source with all our heart, soul, mind, and strength.

Wretchedness—our own wretchedness—must be recognized before true greatness can be properly defined and passionately desired. And it must be recognized not only as a past reality that only memory keeps in view, but also as a present reality that, in all honesty, we must continue to acknowledge.

As I begin to write about what is wrong with us, a thousand pieces of evidence come to mind telling me that whatever is wrong spoils, or at least stains, community. That is its primary effect. Until we have identified a deep, stubborn complex of internal forces whose main effect is to destroy relationships, we have not diagnosed the core problem in human beings. We must see this complex as so hopelessly corrupt that it can only be abandoned and replaced, never repaired. And until we realize that the replacement must come from outside resources, we have not understood the severity of the problem. Whatever is wrong with us makes spiritual community impossible.

Just the other day a friend complained that his car needs new tires but he hasn't time to shop for the best deal. I had received word that morning that I should return to my doctor for more blood tests. I'm traveling six of the next ten days, I'm late on a book deadline (this one), and I have twenty unreturned calls and more than thirty unanswered letters stacked on my desk. As we talked, the thought ran through my mind, *I hope you get a flat tire on your way to work tomorrow.*

But, with restraint and a forced look of interest, I said, "I buy my tires at the Firestone store on Belleview just west of Wadsworth. They give decent service and, I think, fair prices." I felt unengaged as I said it, dull, flat. Nothing more than information came out of me. We left the lunch table, shook hands, and I felt no connection as we parted.

That's Lower Room community. The principle of wretchedness was at work. I saw no evidence of a better power coming out of me. No one struggling with their faith would have observed that interaction and worshiped God.

One more example: A close friend told me on the phone last week that he and his wife are worried about their teenage daughter. They've caught her in a pattern of lies. It's hitting them hard. "Larry," he said with breaking voice, "I don't think I'll ever forget what you said to me a few months ago when we were concerned about our oldest son." He reminded me of the helpful comment. "That one thought has come to mind a dozen times and given me hope each time. It meant the world."

As I began to pray, I was aware of two things stirring inside: a deep love for my friend and his family *and* a desire to say something else memorable. I prayed too long, hoping the Spirit would inspire a powerful phrase and share a bit of the glory with me. Finally, I quit, we expressed genuine, clean love for each other, and hung up. Something alive and good passed between us, but, at least on my part, it was stained. The connection was a hybrid of Lower and Upper Room energy. It always is.

If we are to develop spiritual community, where the healing life of Christ pours out of us and energizes others to give up their self-actualizing demand in favor of knowing Christ, we must understand what else is coming out of us and learn to hate it. Most of us don't really believe that a great principle of wretchedness is in us. We don't think there is a Lower Room in our hearts furnished only with evil passions.

As the impeachment trial of President Bill Clinton ended, one student of the presidency commented, "It's important that people be of good character. But in a real world, all of us are something short of genuinely perfect character."

A professor offered this: "In fairy tales, we know who the heroes and villains are. Little Red Riding Hood is innocent and the wolf is bad. In real life, you get complex characters."

A third observer, this one a historian, put the obvious into words when he said, "So maybe the issue of ethical or moral behavior is less important when people are happy in their own personal lives."[1]

It's typical of Lower Room thinking to deny there is a Lower Room. None of us are distinctly holy or wicked. We're complex. And if things are going well, what does it really matter? We all fall short of hero status, but we can still enjoy our lives. And there are few villains, at least not many that trouble us. As long as Saddam Hussein stays in Iraq and doesn't interfere with my income or tennis game, I don't need to be especially bothered by his evil ways.

But the fact that evil exists is difficult to deny. Newspapers recently focused on a grisly crime that took place in Texas, where three white men dragged a black man for three miles behind a pickup truck. The evening news reported that the leader of this threesome wanted to stage a dramatic event to garner support for his fledgling white supremacy group.

More recently, two boys, one seventeen, the other eighteen, walked into Columbine High School armed with guns and bombs. Before they took their own lives, they killed twelve of their fellow students and one teacher. More than twenty others were wounded, some seriously. It was the worst high school massacre in the history of our country. The Denver community, indeed the nation, will feel the aftershock for years to come.

We need a way of understanding how bearers of a loving God's image, how creatures designed by a good and gracious relational God, can sink to such wretchedness. And we need to search for the means He has provided for restoring the soul to the greatness we may still envision, but rarely experience.

For now, I want to open the door to the Lower Room, walk in, and describe what I see. I'm afraid it's not unlike crawling into a sewer and wading knee-deep in the source of the terrible stench—the stench that rises from dragging a fellow human being three miles behind a pickup truck. The stench that rises from two gunmen opening fire on their classmates. The stench that rises from wishing a friend would have a flat tire.

Let me begin with Pascal's notion of what God might be saying to us. It's a lengthy quote but it's worth the read. It might help us get rid of the idea that wretchedness is evidence of complexity or psychological disturbance and that greatness is the manageable product of good training, effective government, economic advantage, or, if necessary, therapy. Pascal has God saying these words:

> It is I who have made you and I alone can teach you what you are. But you are no longer in the state I made you. I created you holy, innocent, perfect, I filled you with light and understanding, I showed you my glory and my wondrous works. Your eye then beheld the majesty of God. You were not then in the darkness that now blinds your sight, nor subject to death and the miseries that afflict you.
>
> But you could not bear such great glory without falling into presumption. You wanted to make yourself your own center and do without my help. You withdrew from my rule, setting yourself up as my equal in your desire to find happiness in yourself and I abandoned you to yourself.[2]

Pascal then offers his commentary:

> That is the state in which people are today. They retain some feeble
> instinct from the happiness of their first nature [I presume Pascal
> refers to Adam and Eve's nature before that bite of fruit], and are
> plunged into the wretchedness of their blindness and lust which has
> become their second nature [what I call the Lower Room].[3]

If we are to have any real hope of recovering true spiritual community and rescuing the church from the irrelevance of manufactured inspiration and crowd-pleasing entertainment, we must retrieve the lost idea
of a thoroughly evil Lower Room in each of our hearts and see it in ourselves. We must know what to reject as we relate.

The idea was lost in the eighteenth and nineteenth centuries when
a depth view of sin had to be eliminated to keep people excited about
human progress. To maintain Enlightenment-style confidence in our
ability to solve all human problems, we scrapped the idea of a hopelessly corrupt sin nature and reduced flawed morality to voluntary, conscious acts of transgression against known laws, acts that could be
managed.

The remedy became moral instruction, better opportunities, and
accountability, what Dallas Willard calls "sin management." The power
of the Spirit to change life from the inside out was no longer needed.

Notice an important principle: *When sin is lifted up from the bottom
to something less than wretched, virtue is brought down from the top to
something less than great.* Good character was no longer seen as rooted
in worship where a soul was fully engaged with God in humble, broken,
obedient adoration. It rather became little more than social responsibility and a refusal to do bad things. The Holy Spirit was no longer
needed to deal with evil or to develop virtue. Good training and cultural control would do.

With temporal finesse that looks suspiciously devilish, as the church
followed culture in regarding sin as nothing more than voluntary law-
breaking by otherwise fine people, Freud appeared on the scene to offer
a depth view of human distress.

Freud probed deeply into the human psyche and found a labyrinth of dark forces lying beneath our visible problems. He theorized about a Lower Room, secularized it and stripped it of moral stench, and called it the id, a reservoir of energy that if unchecked could lead us into *psychological*, not spiritual, difficulty.

The result was disastrous. While the church became preoccupied with conforming people to moral standards (witness the rise of Fundamentalism in the 1930s), secular probers of our troubled insides took on the task of curing souls.

More recently, large segments of the church have shifted from promoting moral conformity to providing inspiration for living life to the full. In neither case is Lower Room wretchedness meaningfully addressed. Psychotherapists still deal with internal problems according to a de-Christianized principle of human failure and struggle. A Lower Room of moral wretchedness has been theorized out of existence.

Until we recover a distinctly Christian view of what lies beneath eating disorders and multiple personalities and sexual addictions and relational conflict, the value of spiritual community will not be recognized. Churches will continue to heal superficially through moralism, inspirational presentations of relevant truth, and a flurry of wholesome activities. "Tough" cases, those that fail to respond to these efforts, will be referred for professional treatment. Spiritual community will still be viewed as the concern of monastics and contemplatives and not as the calling of all Christians. We'll continue to think of mystics as weird people who sit on top of flagpoles or hide in caves.

Along with a depth view of moral wretchedness, we must also recover a rich understanding of universal priesthood in the church. We're all priests, we all have direct access to God and can draw near to Him, and we all have the life of the Spirit within us waiting to be poured into others. And it is that life that can heal the soul. The community of God, as it journeys to God, has all the resources within its members to keep us moving. We simply need to become a community, to get together as a joined and closely knit body, to connect with one another.

I want now to suggest a way of thinking about both our wretchedness, which may help us recover a depth view of sin, and our greatness, which may encourage us to live like priests. We're now in the Lower Room. Let's look around. We need to get a good look at the room in each of us that, when seen, will be hated, eventually abandoned, and ultimately destroyed.

CHAPTER 9

Lower Room
Furnishings

[Referring to Alexander Whyte, Presbyterian pastor of the nineteenth
century:] He brought me face to face with a characteristic of Puritanism
which I had almost forgotten. For him, one essential symptom of the
regenerate life is a permanent and permanently horrified perception of
one's natural and (it seems) unalterable corruption. The true
Christian's nostril is to be continually attentive to the cesspool

—C. S. Lewis

On August 27, 1996, three weeks before his unexpected death, Henri
Nouwen wrote these words in his journal:

We who offer spiritual leadership often find ourselves not living
what we are preaching or teaching. It is not easy to avoid hypocrisy
completely because we find ourselves saying things larger than ourselves. I often call people to a life I am not fully able to live myself.
[And then he added:] I am learning that the best cure for hypocrisy
is community. Hypocrisy is not so much the result of not living what
I preach but much more of not confessing my inability to fully live
up to my own words.[1]

Like each of us, Nouwen simply *couldn't* be everything he should be.

I have been reflecting lately on C. S. Lewis's metaphor of ghosts and solid people from *The Great Divorce*. Ghosts from hell, as Lewis tells the story, took a bus trip to the outskirts of heaven and were each confronted by an angel who explained to them that they were wrongly trusting in one thing or another to make them whole. To become persons who could enjoy the environment of heaven—*solid* persons—they would have to give up their poorly placed trust. Those who refused remained ghosts.

To become a solid person, I must give up whatever idols I am depending on to give me life. Those idols may be a son or daughter, a career, a reputation, a special relationship either ongoing or lost, or a superficial lifestyle that helps me avoid conflict.

These idols are not doing the job. Rather than making me whole, they leave me empty, ghostlike. But I must be *persuaded* of that before I will give them up. And the only way to persuade me is to convince me that they are not giving me what I most deeply want. Now the hard truth is that I will not be convinced apart from suffering—a kind of suffering that lets me see that these gods have not touched the parts of my heart that suffering exposes. Therefore, I must suffer.

When I suffer, I focus better. I realize that something like a new car is nice, and perhaps a legitimate purchase, but it will not feed my soul. Suffering brings into focus what my soul most deeply yearns for and I am directed to God. I learn to depend on Him. But even as I write these words, I am saying things larger than myself. Throughout this entire book, I am calling you to a life I am not fully able to live myself.

I remember one of the times I was a ghost for another person. It made me realize that when someone leans on a ghost, both fall over.

Some years back, a friend's daughter had just run away from home, his wife admitted to an affair, and his mother died, all within the space of one week.

He called me and asked to spend some time with me. Within a day of the call, he flew to Colorado and we spent nearly a week together. Part of the time we played. We saw two movies, took in the auto show, and ate several steaks together.

This was a man who had mildly offended me several years before his string of tragedies occurred. We had never dealt with it. I doubt if he even knew how I felt, and I was too ashamed to own up to how foolishly sensitive I had been. But as we talked, I couldn't shake a nagging sense that the thing to do was point out how he had neglected his daughter and failed his wife and perhaps was poorly handling his mother's death. *Where did that urge come from?* Even as I wept with him, I remember feeling mean-spirited. A small part of me seemed unable to fully resist wanting to hurt this man.

We talked, I did my best to encourage him and, more by being with him than by offering wisdom, I tried to further whatever the Spirit was doing in him through his hard time. He returned home and we lost contact with each other.

Recently, I was planning a trip to his part of the country and called to arrange a visit. We met for lunch and after some friendly catch-up conversation, he said, "You know, I really don't want to tell you how I'm doing. When I spent that week with you a few years back, I left feeling criticized. You don't feel like a safe person for me."

Why, at the end of his life, did Henri Nouwen feel smaller than his message? Why do I feel smaller than mine? More to the point, why *am* I smaller? What is wrong with each of us that keeps us living like unsafe ghosts in a world that longs for solid people?

Let me begin to answer those questions with this: What was wrong with Lewis and Nouwen is the same thing that's wrong with you and me. And it's the same thing that was wrong with Hitler and Stalin.

I call it the Lower Room. Lewis called it a cesspool. The Bible calls it the *flesh.* "The New Testament designates the total organization of sin by the term *sarx* (flesh), referring to the fallen human personality apart from the renewing influence and control of the Holy Spirit."[2] Listen to Richard Lovelace highlight the message of Jonathan Edwards's sermon, *Men Naturally God's Enemies:*

> Although most human beings give the appearance at times of being
> confused seekers for truth with a naive respect for God, the reality
> is that unless they are moved by the Spirit they have a natural dis-
> taste for the real God, an *uncontrollable* [emphasis mine] desire to

break his laws and a constant tendency to sit in judgment on him when they notice him at all. Since his purposes cross theirs at every juncture, they really hate him more than any finite object, and this is clearly displayed in their treatment of his Son. They are largely unconscious of this enmity. It is usually repressed through their unbelief, their creation of agreeable false portraits of God, their sense of his distance from us, their fear of punishment or their lack of awareness of the magnitude of their guilt.[3]

Imagine trying to put together a community with people like that. That's exactly what we've all been doing since Adam and Eve tried to put together the first family. It didn't work then and it's not working now.

It's easy to lose sight (sometimes never to gain it) of how bad we are. When we understand that the Spirit of God has created a wonderful room in our souls full of light and singing and love, we sometimes discount the power of the bad room that's also still there. It helps us feel better about ourselves. We like to think we're rather decent folks, a few quirks here and there, maybe even clay feet, but with nothing really *evil* about us.

The architect of the Lower Room likes nothing better. If we can't smell the cesspool within us, we'll be less bothered by it. We'll be more likely to bathe in it, thinking the water is reasonably clean.

But a Lower Room exists in each of us, and it is *bad*. Even though we may sincerely try to connect with each other in the fragrant ambiance of the Upper Room, we so often manage to speak a word from our Lower Room that spoils things, that makes our community unspiritual, that makes us more ghostlike than solid. And then, as we saw a few chapters ago, when conflict comes we retreat behind congeniality, get together by cooperating on worthy projects, ask special friends for mere consolation, or, if the conflict is severe, we seek counseling or submit ourselves to conforming pressure.

But we've too quickly moved to solutions before properly understanding the problem. A clear description of the problem may help us see how inadequate our solutions are, and it may prompt more interest in God's radical and—even among Christians—largely ignored solution.

Teresa of Avila tells us that our problem is like "snakes and vipers and poisonous creatures" that slither around the outskirts of the splendid castle that is our regenerate soul.[4] She counsels us to begin our journey to God by developing self-knowledge that humbles us. I think she means for us to see the snakes in the Lower Room and to be so frightened by them that we eagerly run toward the Upper Room, which she calls Seventh Mansions.

C. S. Lewis takes it a step further by telling us there are two varieties of snakes. He distinguishes between two kinds of sin, each one coming from a separate corrupted part of our selves, what I think of as first-floor and cellar sins.

> The sins of the flesh are bad, but they are the least bad of all sins. All the worst pleasures are purely spiritual: the pleasure of putting other people in the wrong, . . . the pleasures of power, of hatred. For there are two things inside me, competing with the human self which I must try to become. They are the Animal Self and the Diabolical Self. The Diabolical Self is the worse of the two. That is why a cold, self-righteous prig who goes regularly to church may be far nearer to hell than a prostitute.[5]

The *partial* brokenness that comes from facing the horror of first-floor sins will not release us to become a part of spiritual community. *Deep* brokenness is required, the kind that comes from feeling the snakes crawl over our naked feet as we stand in the cellar, from smelling the stench of our interior cesspool.

If we repent of first-floor sins without feeling disgust over cellar sins, we'll make little progress toward maturity. We'll become the self-righteous prig who goes regularly to church but never contributes to spiritual community.

Permit a personal illustration of that last point. Right now I'm sitting on an airplane, United Flight 263, still at the gate in Chicago, nearly ready to push back and carry me to Denver. Today's trip began in Milwaukee where yesterday I presented a seminar on spiritual community.

The seminar went well. The Spirit moved.

I've learned to be wary right after a good spiritual experience. I tend to feel more vulnerable then to temptation that, at other times, I easily resist. A pastor once told me that after a particularly powerful sermon he feels a strange compulsion to tell someone a dirty joke. I know what he means.

When my new friend John dropped me at the Milwaukee airport earlier this morning, I had about twenty minutes to kill before boarding. With a bucket of coffee already swirling through my stomach, I happily passed by Starbucks and headed for the bookstore. I was pleasantly surprised. It was a used bookstore, well stocked, good prices. I had never seen one in an airport before. I immediately saw the sign "Classic Fiction" and walked to the aisle it marked.

Feeling like a chocoholic at Ghiradelli's on the San Francisco wharf, I feasted my eyes on volumes by Dickens, Dorothy Sayers, and O'Henry.

And then something happened. As I scanned the top shelf for more treasures, I caught sight of another sign marking another, nearly adjacent, aisle. The sign read "Erotica."

It was a knee-jerk reaction. My Animal Self instantly urged me to take the walk.

For about twenty seconds, my taste for Dickens died. I knew the urge was wrong. But it was a first-floor urge and, as I reckoned with it, I was partially broken. I made the deliberate, difficult choice to bring my eyes back down to what felt less appealing, to the classic fiction titles. I spotted Walker Percy's *The Thanatos Syndrome*, bought it for $3.95 and, like Joseph fleeing Potiphar's wife, I hurried to my departure gate.

As I boarded the plane, I remember feeling proud, not grateful, but *proud*. Lots of men, maybe even some preachers, might have yielded, lost track of time in the Erotica aisle, and missed their plane. With satisfaction, I flipped open Percy's book and began reading as we took off for Chicago.

I had entered the ring and knocked out my Animal Self. That was good. But I didn't see my Diabolical Self sitting ringside grinning broadly. At that moment, I was a ghost, feeding my soul on *pride*. The emptiness remained. Perhaps, in my mind, my noble moralism made me deserving of a little more respect from my students when I next taught them, or of extra appreciation from my wife and friends.

The snakes were crawling, the stench from the cesspool was rising, and I thought I had just splashed on cologne. In that condition, I could do nothing but contribute to unspiritual community. Cellar sins were spreading their poison.

But exactly what are these "cellar sins"?

First, a caution. As I write about the furnishings in this lowest level of our Lower Room, I ask you to do the hard work of personalizing what you read. It will do us no good if we discuss badness that we think is someone else's problem. We will find no help if we approach the discussion as merely curious students of the soul, as observers of people in general who manage to keep an academic distance away from what is in us that should make us vomit.

There are, I think, *four furnishings* in our Lower Room, four distinguishable passions, each of which is a corruption of something good. Let me first list them, then discuss them.

The Four Furnishings of Our Lower Room

1. The corrupted *image of God* that fills us with a *passion for self.*
2. The corrupted *resources* we've been given as human beings that fill us with a *passion for control.*
3. Pleasurable and painful *life experiences* that we corrupt by responding to them with a *passion to define life* (pleasures we must reexperience) and *death* (pain we must avoid).
4. The corruption of *God's holy law* that was given to reveal our need but now stimulates a *passion to perform* that literally drives us mad.

Furnishing #1: A Passion for Self
(The Corruption of the Image of God)

The first thing we meet in the Lower Room is a desire to relate that has been twisted into something utterly self-preoccupying. This, I believe, is the very heart of our Diabolical Self. Lewis once lamented, in speaking of his dying wife, that "all this is fleshly rhetoric about loving you. I never had a selfless thought since I was born. I am mercenary and self-seeking through and through."

A close friend called last night, asking me to pray. He and his wife just learned that their son, a straight-A student, leader-of-the-youth-group kind of guy enrolled in a Christian college, is hooked on cocaine. I couldn't entirely smother the thought, *I'm glad this isn't my son.* The snake was crawling up my leg.

We ask, no, we *demand* that everything in life serve our purpose, at least that it take our well-being into account. The energy of our Lower Room is radically and unalterably self-centered. Nothing more severely violates the pattern of Trinitarian relating.

If we bend low enough, we might hear the rumblings coming from this awful passion. At every moment, in every relationship, we're asking questions or saying things like this, if not out loud then at least under our breath:

- She didn't smile at me when I came into the room. I wonder if she's mad at me. She can really be snooty.

- Why doesn't he call? I've left three messages. Oh well, no one really cares about me anyhow.

- He never comes to visit.

- This is a pretty bright bunch of people. I better keep my opinions to myself.

- You think you've got it bad? Do you want to hear what I've been through?

- I can't believe you're doing this to me. This will make my life so much more difficult.

Our culture has convinced us that these are the rumblings of insecurity, not selfishness, and that people who say or think such things need psychological help rather than spiritual renewal. But these are evidences of personal corruption, not bad backgrounds or low self-esteem.

We still bear the image of God. We want to belong to a community, to be intimate with people, to enjoy each other. And we can't stop wanting these things. It's what we were made for. But our desires have been corrupted. Now we're no longer radically other-centered, we're fundamentally self-centered. Our *capacity* for relationship has become a desperate *longing* for relationship that quickly translates into an indignant *demand* for relationship. I need love, so *love me!*

We're like children who refuse to eat at our wealthy father's table and run instead into the streets, first begging for, then demanding, and eventually stealing food from someone else. The corrupted image of God now impassions us to want, above all else, a community where others relate well *to us*.

It seems reasonable and right. The *first thing* of loving God and others has become nudged aside by the *second thing* of receiving love (what we define as love) from others. Self-worship, disguised as embracing our longings, setting our boundaries, and taking care of ourselves has become our first thing.

Furnishing #2: A Passion to Control
(The Corruption of Our God-Given Resources to Subdue the Earth)

The second reality that greets us as we descend into the cellar of our Lower Room is a *determination,* a resolve that presents itself as both noble and necessary. Strongly imbedded in our natural self (which is diabolical) is a commitment to depend on the resources we've been given to make life turn out the way we want it to.

Resources that were designed for good purposes are now used for bad ones. Money is spent, not to sustain healthy life and provide community-building recreation, but to make us feel important. I suspect we might have enough money to feed every starving child in the world if advertising didn't strike such a deep chord within us. How different things might be if we could recognize real soul food and distinguish it from pride food.

Like every corrupted passion, this one feeds on the Big Lie, that no one cares about us as we care about ourselves. Oswald Chambers once said that the root of all sin is the suspicion that God isn't good, that He really doesn't care about what matters most to us.

We feel our longing to relate, we reflexively reduce that longing to a demand that others relate well to us, and, because no one else cares whether we're properly loved or not, we take on the job of seeing to it that we get what we need.

When someone hurts us, our priority shifts from getting what we need to protecting ourselves from further pain. Sometimes the best and quickest way to feel alive is to hate a person who rejected us. Hate feels powerful. It requires others to take us into account. We may be rejected, but our presence will still be felt.

We devote our most creative energies to developing self-enhancing or self-protective *strategies of relating*. We come up with ways of interacting with others that have a reasonable chance of prodding others to give us what we want, ways that keep us safe in case they don't.

For example, think how we may use a sense of humor or a quick mind. The ability to laugh and make others laugh is a gift from God. But it can be used by husbands to deflect serious conversation with their wives, conversations that may lead to conflict and disappointment.

A quick mind can be put to similar use.

Wife: "Why didn't you call me to say you would be late?"
Husband: "Is the problem here really trust? I hate feeling that every day I have to prove to you that I'm not a bad guy. Yes, I was late and yes, I didn't call. But you know what I'd like? Just once, I'd like it if you were to wonder if maybe I am coming home tired from working so late to support my family. Is that asking too much?"

A friend said to me three days ago that he is afraid to offer his thoughts to me about counseling. Sometimes I probe his thoughts with a spirit that conveys to him "You really don't have much to offer, at least not to me." It may be his issue, but I suspect we've met too often in the basement to have our dialogues.

This second furnishing comes closest to what the Bible calls the *flesh,* that reservoir of energy that will never bow the knee to God and is determined to find a way to experience life without Him.

Furnishing #3: A Passion to Define
(The Corruption of "Life Experiences" into an
Opportunity to Decide What to Live for and What to
Avoid, to Define Life and Death for Our Souls)

We simply cannot handle the burden of deciding what is worth living for. We get it wrong every time.

God has already told us to live for Him, to be like Him, to represent Him to others, and to further His plans. When we turn away from His ideas, we turn instead to our experiences in life to see what is good and bad. Whatever feels good, what seems to give us an immediate experience of life, we decide *is* life; we decide it is food for our souls, and we chase after it with all the excitement of a street person in the back alley rummaging through the fine restaurant's garbage.

And whatever feels bad, what makes us quickly miserable, we decide is death, and we develop a game plan to keep from experiencing it again. Suffering is to be avoided or at least minimized.

When we're abused or rejected or criticized, we don't look at these painful experiences as reason to more clearly depend on God and demonstrate His character in the midst of them. Instead, they become the basis for our figuring out how to live. We *interpret* life experiences, we process them to see how various things make us feel so we can make important decisions about how to live. It's a bit like dating. Check out the field to see what kind of person might make you happy. If you make a bad decision, you can always back out and try again.

I recently asked my counseling students to write down one painful experience and one happy one.

Frank remembered the time his dad thought he wasn't pulling his weight on an assigned task, so he hit Frank, who was twelve years old at the time, hard enough to knock him out.

I wonder how Frank learned to define death. We let bad life experiences define death rather than hearing God's thoughts on the matter. Perhaps Frank has dedicated his life to never falling short, or to never being *perceived* as falling short, on a job that someone else watches him tackle. That might have shaped Frank into a guarded person, into someone who tackles very little, into someone who is terrified, for instance, to work hard at his marriage and family. I wonder if he lives with both terror and fear around his wife: She might want him to be a real father, he might fail, at least in her eyes, and then she would get mad at him.

That would not be spiritual community.

Another student wrote about the time he brought his adopted daughter home from the hospital, a moment of great joy. But if he has assumed the responsibility for defining life, that moment could lead in troublesome directions: "I am alive when someone needs me, when I can feel strong and necessary and depended on."

His daughter might grow up feeling dangerous. "I can give life to my dad or I can take it away." She will hate the power, and might use it to keep her dad intact by becoming a very good girl or to destroy him by rebelling.

Neither would be spiritual community.

Our passion to define life and death always misleads us. We were never meant to possess the knowledge of good and evil.

Now, before I add the last furnishing, consider what we have so far: a selfish person, determined to get what he wants, who always goes after the wrong thing. Put a few of these people together and you will not experience spiritual community, ever.

What does God do? He looks down on all the corruption, He sees all the bickering and backbiting, and He says, "Stop it! Here's what you should be doing." And He gives us the Law, a series of commandments and principles that, if we follow them, will make us happy and join us together in spiritual community. He thunders from Sinai.

But no one does what He says. Some of us try, but we can't quite get it right. Even if we don't care what He says, we have the idea floating in our heads that there must be a better way to go about this business of living. Whatever we sense might be better, we try to do it. But we can't do that quite right either. We all end up feeling pressured. We can't get away from the passion to perform. And that's the last passion in our Lower Room.

Furnishing #4: A Passion to Perform
(The Corruption of Moral Absolutes into Pressure to Do Right Rather than Letting Moral Absolutes Produce Gratitude for Grace, for Love Even When We Fail)

Tell a person driving himself to the hospital with kidney stone pain to stop at the stop sign and he'll scream at you. That's what we do to God.

- "How dare you tell me to go back to that man? Don't You know how he's hurt me?"

- "Be thankful? For what? Look, my son needs braces, I can't afford them, and my ex won't help. And I'm supposed to be thankful?"

- "Not take my girlfriend to bed? You've got to be kidding. Life is hard. I've had a lot of rejection. This girl wants me. I'm going for it."

The trouble is that we know God is right, and we can't entirely quiet our conscience. Like preachers who pound their pulpits when their point is weak, we angrily declare our freedom from any pressure to measure up to someone else's standards, especially God's. We "wail on our beds" (see Hos. 7:14) about how much we hurt, thinking that surely our level of internal pain justifies whatever we must do to find relief.

The shift toward postmodern thinking encourages our attitude. Large segments of our culture have decided to throw off the pressure of holiness, to abolish absolutes, to honor whatever seems right to the individual. Postmodernism didn't introduce the idea of abolishing absolute truth and law, it only dignified it, or tried to. Now it's immoral to honor any authority outside of ourselves.

The battle is fierce. But it's a battle against that nagging sense of morality, that irritating fear that what we're doing is really sinful. When someone comes and tells us we're wrong, as Jesus did, we kill him.

Everything I've just said can be summarized in a sketch using the familiar image of an iceberg. Above the water line is whatever visible problems trouble us. Below is the Lower Room, the source of all the trouble. The contents of the Lower Room might be called Flesh Dynamics.

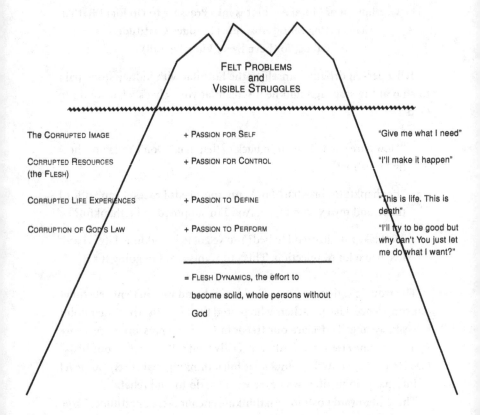

There's the mess, the smelly cesspool, the slithering serpents. How can we build spiritual community with these passions ruling our lives? We can't.

But God has a plan. And, not surprisingly, it's a surprise, and a really good one. It can lead us to spiritual community. We'll discuss the plan in the next chapter.

CHAPTER 10

There *Is* an
Upper Room

A man cannot think too little of his self, or too much
of his soul.—G. K. Chesterton

Sometimes there is no greater act of faith than to believe there is something fundamentally good in the Christian people we live with.
Especially ourselves. We can all be so petty, so defensive, so committed
to making our point and having our way. And we can masterfully dis-
guise our wretched commitments as great efforts to advance God's kingdom. Think back to the last church committee meeting you attended.
Did anyone really *hear* anyone else? Was anyone humble enough to
explore another's viewpoint and then to change his mind about something important? Have you done that? Have I?

In spiritual community, people participate in dialogue: They share
without manipulation, they listen without prejudice, they decide without self-interest. The absence of dialogue is sure evidence that we don't
really believe others are speaking from a place worth hearing, and it is
even stronger proof that we ourselves, whatever we may think, are not
in fact speaking from that place. Our words are so often unwholesome,
not the edifying words we're told to speak (Eph. 4:29).

A Christian worldview provides reason for us to respect each other, to expect to learn from every encounter with a fellow image bearer. Only in Christianity is there a clear basis for regarding each other as having profound worth.

Christians believe that within every person, something exists of inestimable value. The Bible calls it a soul, an *eternal* soul. Dorothy Sayers says somewhere that hell is God's greatest compliment to man. Dogs and cats don't go to hell. *People* do—creatures whose capacity for personal, self-conscious joy means they also are cursed with the capability of experiencing misery of the worst kind, loneliness, self-hatred, and aimlessness.

Whether we eventually (and eternally) experience joy or misery depends on how we view our soul and whether we feed it Christ or something else. That's true for every person. But for every *Christian* person, the soul can be viewed not only as valuable but also as *good*. The Christian's soul is regenerated, made alive with the actual life passed back and forth among the members of the Trinity. It is that good *life*, which I call the Upper Room.

Because it never comes naturally, I regard it as a great triumph when the first impulse in my counseling students as they hear a counselee's concern is to look, not for what's *wrong* with the person, but for what's *right*. The overriding focus in a spiritual conversation is not on sin or psychological damage but on the Spirit's movement. What's good? Where is the goodness? We know it's there, perhaps hidden, but it's always present. What evidence can we find of the Spirit's creative involvement in each other's life? *That's* the focus of spiritual community.

Think of the members of your small group. Go around the room. Peggy dominates every conversation with spiritual bromides that make you ill. Her husband is rich, her children beautiful, her figure, thanks to a personal trainer, is trim. When Suzanne, the chubby wife of a plumber shares how depressed she feels over how badly her kids are doing in school, Peggy gushes, "Oh honey, you've just got to turn them over to Jesus. He loves them so much more than even you do. It'll all be okay. Just stay in Jesus' presence."

Marshall smiles a lot. Prying a reflective comment out of him would be harder than opening the lid on a child-proof prescription bottle. He is the last person you would tell about your struggle with lust.

Marlene, when you let her, takes up much of the group's time sharing her struggles. You wonder if she ever has a good day, if she ever feels happy. Mel, the group's outspoken cynic, once told her to get a life. The tension between them has been palpable in every meeting since.

And Gary. He likes to discuss how rich his quiet times are becoming. The first time you heard it, you felt drawn. The tenth time didn't excite you as much.

How on earth can this group ever approach spiritual community? Is the first step to lay everything on the table, to clear the air and surface the conflict?

"Peggy, you feel so shallow to me. It's too easy for you to talk about Jesus' love. Your life is a storybook fantasy."

"Suzanne, you need to lose thirty pounds."

"Marshall, have you ever had a real thought? Your bland smile drives me crazy."

"Marlene, you aren't the only one with problems! You are so self-absorbed."

"Mel, I never feel tenderness from you. You seem so angry and biting."

"Gary, stop parading your spirituality. You're not a desert father, you know."

Opening the door to our Lower Rooms and releasing whatever's inside is not healthy honesty. It requires the wrong kind of courage.

Courage, Nouwen notes, comes from *coeur*, which means "heart." "To have courage is to listen to our heart, to speak from our heart, and to give from our heart."[1] But our heart has two chambers, an upper and a lower room. Speaking from the Lower Room requires *fleshly* courage, self-assertion, the freedom to speak my mind and not care what you think. That's very different from spiritual courage, from speaking out of our Upper Room.

For that to happen, someone needs to see the Upper Room in Peggy and Marshall and Mel, and to discover their own. Members of a spiritual community look at each other with the conviction that God has placed something terrific in every member. It may be well hidden, but spiritual energy can see it, call it forth, and enjoy it.

When that happens, it's a miracle, a *convincing* miracle. Jesus told us that the world would believe Him when that miracle occurred. Spiritual community is always a miracle. It never happens without the Spirit.

For example, a good marriage is a miracle for which only God can claim credit. Long ago, I passed the point where I've lived with my wife longer than with my parents. No one knows me as well as she. Perhaps our greatest battle, and at the same time our richest blessing, has been to see the Upper Room in each other. We've had thirty-three years, and counting, to find it.

Rachael provides me with the Safety of Hope. I have the confidence that nothing she discovers about me will shake her confidence that, literally by God's grace, I am fundamentally a good man. Should I have an affair, there would be grave consequences, perhaps divorce if I continued in sinful ways, but somewhere deep within her being she would still regard me as a good man. It's that goodness that would make an affair so tragic, so abnormally grotesque. Pigs grovel in mud. People take baths. When people join the pigs, something is wrong.

When I believe that you believe I am a good man, I don't tend toward arrogance or presumption. I rest. And in my rest, I am more able to face my Diabolical Self and to then discover and celebrate my Celestial Self. What do we believe about each other, not only when we're on our best behavior, but when we're irritating and demanding?

Thomas à Kempis once wrote, "It is not easy to live in a Religious Community."[2] He was referring to monastic life but what he said is true for any group of Christians who long for rich spiritual connection. We're all so imperfect and closeness to one another makes it obvious. Yet distance is the wrong solution. He then added, "It is the complete mortification of passions that make a True Religious." But is that the right solution? My answer is a loud NO!

Spiritual people not only mortify bad passions ("I will not yield to my urge to criticize my brother"), they also celebrate and freely indulge good ones ("I respect him so much; I'm going to tell him"). They discover an Upper Room in their redeemed hearts where there are no snakes, only flowers and sunsets and majestic mountains and cool springs of living water.

It is true, of course, that the Spirit often exposes the furnishings of our Lower Room. But He does so only to help us appreciate the wonder of Christ and to find the Upper Room He has built in our hearts. He wants us to actually feel the energy of godly, holy, clean passions swirling through our inmost being.

There *is* an Upper Room, but I'm beginning to think that if we try to experience its passions without first smelling the reek of our Lower Room, we will discover only *natural* virtue, what is really only socialized sin that still comes from the Lower Room. We will be deceived by the effect of air freshener liberally sprayed over garbage.

I also believe that no one can help me locate my Upper Room without having confidence that it's there. Only then will I feel safe. Realistically appraising the evil in my Lower Room is terrifying. As I uncover what's bad within me, a spiritual friend stays relaxed. He sees something else. I know of little else so powerful as confessing wretched failure and having a friend look on you with great delight.

I had the privilege of being that friend two days ago. Someone I know sinned grievously and told me about it. We not only celebrated forgiveness together; we also enjoyed his realization that continuing in that sin was not what he wanted to do. In his inner being, he delighted in God's law (Rom. 7:22). I felt what a surgeon must feel when he looks at a cancer patient's x-ray and, with a smile, says, "There's enough healthy tissue here for an excellent prognosis. You need surgery but you'll soon be better than ever."

The more I see my sin in the presence of a spiritual community, the more I see Christ and celebrate Him and long to know Him and be like Him. The safety necessary to own my badness comes when someone believes that I am in Christ and that He is in me. Then anything can be faced without fear of being discarded. The point is important. Permit an illustration.

For several years, I was aware of a wrong feeling within me, a passion toward a few people that was about as winsome as a black widow spider, and equally deadly. I begged God to renew in me a clean spirit, to shower mercy on me and to pour out His love so fully into my soul that nothing else would spill out. I longed to know, in the old Puritan expression, "the expulsive power of a new affection."

When I made known this struggle to a good friend, he didn't trace its roots or interpret its meaning or command me to change. Instead, his eyes moistened as he said, "I am so drawn to Christ because of you. It is so wonderful to see how much you hate whatever comes between you and our Lord." He saw my Upper Room, the healthy tissue mixed in with the bad. He recognized the principle of greatness at work, even when the principle of wretchedness was far more visible.

I've told that story before. It happened three years ago. Here's the sequel. Because of people like that in my life, I sometimes feel safe. Thanks to how they see me, I more deeply *know* that I am in Christ, that nothing soiled, or even mildly stained, can stand in His presence. And I am there. And I more fully *know* that Christ is in me, that beneath every base desire there is a robust appetite for holiness.

Only when these truths are positioned in our minds will an overwhelming revelation of the depths of our depravity provoke not despair but worship. Only then will it cement these truths in place. A vision of what is wonderful must precede the disruption of facing what's awful. I speak from recent experience.

It was two in the morning. Suddenly I sat bolt upright in bed, as if a fire alarm had sounded. An image so loathsome I cannot describe it had, entirely unbidden, entered my mind and filled it. I could think of nothing else.

I remember saying to myself, "I have been taken to hell."

A noiseless scream, louder within me than if it had escaped my lips, rose out of my depths: "I am in Christ! I do not belong here. I am covered by His blood, forgiven, seated in heavenly places. What am I doing here? *This is not where I belong!*"

For perhaps twenty minutes (I really don't know how long) the spiritual agony continued unabated. The odious image stayed clear. And then, the most definite sense came upon me. It came from outside. It was not me talking to myself. Of that I am certain.

The sense (I almost said *voice,* and that would be nearly correct), more than anything else, was gentle. With ears that were not physical, I heard someone say, "*This* is where your anger comes from," referring to the hellish image.

Of course it was a rebuke, a judgment, but it seemed more like an invitation. It was *gentle,* so very gentle. I had no doubt the speaker of those words loved me. I had never before heard such ugly truth spoken with such unlimited love.

I immediately relaxed. The anguish was gone, the image vanished, replaced in one stroke by immense peace. I had been lifted to a different place. As I meditated on the experience, it seemed as if God had held me by the feet and, with a secure grip, dipped me into the cesspool till I was overcome by the stench, then lifted me into an Upper Room. I was instantly taken to the communion table with Jesus and His friends. I could see the people I had mercilessly judged sitting near Jesus, each one mercifully unjudged and warmly enjoyed.

That brief spiritual journey took me from mere awareness of my Upper Room to a vivid experience of my Lower Room. That, in turn, transformed my *knowledge* of good things within me into an actual experience. I tasted the Lord and saw He was good and, miracle of miracles, I tasted His goodness in me.

I *wanted* to forgive and ask forgiveness. It was no longer a requirement but a privilege, something I now longed to do. I took appropriate action the next day. Because someone believed that Christ was in me, I faced the enormity of my sin and emerged with hope. I had been carried to a better place.

Before I take you on a tour of the Upper Room, I must tell you that, so far, this is proving to be the most difficult chapter I have written. At the same time, it is the easiest. Let me explain. I was hit in the stomach again this morning with another example of how prone I am to "connect" with others from my Lower Room and to see only that room in others.

A few men critical of my ministry asked to meet with me. I rose early this morning to pray. Before I left my place of sanctuary, I sang the hymn "Christ Liveth in Me." The second verse reduced me to tears. It reads like this:

As rays of light from yonder sun the flow'rs of earth set free,
So life and light and love come forth from Christ living in me.

I *believe* those words. I long to *live* those words. I begged God to release the life of Christ within me toward my critics.

I'm writing now a few hours after the meeting. It seemed to me more like congenial relating, with some tense moments, than connecting. I had a hard time seeing their Upper Room. Their kindness felt natural, not supernatural, more an effort to keep things pleasant than a perseveringly gracious spirit in the midst of trouble.

And I sensed an edge rising within me at several points when the substantive disagreements were approached. I wanted to speak candidly with a gentle, open-to-dialogue-but-here's-where-I-am spirit, but I couldn't. I could fake it, but Lower Room energy seemed stronger in me than the better kind. I not only differ with their position on several matters, but I think I see bad motives beneath their viewpoint. I could see nothing better in them. And that fact seemed more clear to me at the time than the fact that Lower Room passions were seeping out of me.

That experience of missed connection discourages me. I'm reminded of Nouwen's words that I am writing about things larger than myself, a life I am not fully able to live. Do any of us ever live it? How close do we come? How close *can* we come? Some relationships just won't work. We have to accept that. We have to live as peaceably as we can with many, while we develop spiritual community with a few.

Those thoughts make it difficult to write about our beautiful Upper Room, the unpolluted source of deep connecting. But I perceive another reality, one that makes it easy, even fun, to write about the Upper Room. I *have* tasted spiritual community, not perfect spiritual community but truly spiritual nonetheless.

The family time of worship I spoke of earlier in this book comes quickly to mind. I've also enjoyed dozens of conversations that bore the unmistakable imprint of God's Spirit. Some followed serious conflict, like the healing conversations I had with a close friend after we had screamed at each other walking the streets of Chicago. Thanks to continued involvement with him, I can see his Upper Room. It's resplendent. I hope he can see mine. I believe he does.

I know something of God is alive in me, and I have felt the impact of that same aliveness in others. Just ten minutes ago, I hung up the phone after a good chat with a mentor. His final words were, "I'm proud of you, Larry. I really am." I had made known no recent achievement or special virtue. He somehow caught a whiff of Christ in me and let me know he enjoyed the fragrance. The life within me was stirred. I felt safe, seen, and touched. That's *spiritual* community.

There *is* another room. And it's wonderful. We take our tour in the next chapter.

CHAPTER 11

Upper Room
Furnishings

The world thinks men are good and saints are better. Pascal knows men
are sinners and saints are miracles.—Peter Kreeft

Perhaps the best starting point for our tour of the Upper Room is the
vision God many years ago gave to Teresa of Avila. Listen to her words:

> I began to think of the soul as if it were a castle made up of a sin-
> gle diamond or of very clear crystal. Now if we think carefully over
> this, sisters, the soul of the righteous man is nothing but a paradise.
> I can find nothing with which to compare the great beauty of a soul
> and its great capacity.[1]

To capture the drama of God's work in the soul and to see how it over-
turns everything natural in our relationships, let me ask you to think of
someone who right now is worrying you. Perhaps it is a loved one who
knows Christ but has been hardened by recent trials. As you read this
chapter, understand that I am not asking you to think well of this person, or even charitably, but to think truthfully, accurately, realistically.
You've seen their Lower Room. Can you now see the upper one?

Let me describe it. As I did with the Lower Room, I will first list *four furnishings* of the Upper Room, then I will discuss each one.

The Four Furnishings of Our Upper Room
(What Teresa Called the Seventh Mansions)

1. The renewed image of Christ with its *passion to worship,* a desire, unrivaled in potential strength, to glorify God by enjoying Him and revealing Him to others.
2. A recognition of who we are and who God is that stirs a *passion to trust,* a passion that makes it possible to rest in a storm and continue, quietly, our journey to God, a passion to radically depend on God.
3. An attitude that views life experiences as an opportunity to satisfy a *passion to grow* and as reason to celebrate trials as spiritually forming, and blessings as foretastes of what's ahead.
4. An embracing of God's law as the character of the Person we most love that fuels a *passion to obey,* not a pressure but an anger-free, supernaturally aroused eagerness to please our Father.

In order to speak clearly about these furnishings, we need first to realize something about the gospel of Jesus Christ that is commonly overlooked.

In chapter 9, I suggested that God has looked at the mess we have made of our lives. He has seen our self-focused desires, our stubborn independence, our foolish definition of "life as pleasure now" and of "death as pain now." He has said, "The way you are living life is wrong. Here's the right way to live. Now do it!"

When God wrote the Ten Commandments in stone, He established what the Bible later calls the Old Covenant. The Old Covenant was an agreement God made with people. It was simple: Do right and you live. Do wrong and you die. He meant what He said. Our obligation was to do *completely* right, to obey every command all the time and to obey it perfectly.

Two consequences followed this covenant.

One, we didn't keep our end of the bargain; no one did. No one *could,* so we died. We were all condemned to die as law-breakers, to remain separate from the source of everything good.

Two, we got mad. The agreement seemed unfair, a setup for God to hate us. We couldn't live up to His ridiculously high standards, especially not when we've been related to so poorly by God and everyone else. God seemed insensitive to how difficult life was and to how reasonable we were in demanding relief.

The law, then, not only pronounced us guilty, it also aroused our sinful Lower Room passions. We felt more justified in finding someone to love us as we define love, more determined to depend on ourselves to make life work, and more focused on pursuing what we decided was life. The workings of Flesh Dynamics intensified. God's giving of the Law made things worse.

Then, when He decided it was time, He did what He had planned all along and had hinted at all through Jewish history. He threw out the Old Covenant and made a new one. The Old Covenant was never intended to solve our problem but to reveal it, to reveal our need for a different plan.

This *New* Covenant, what we more familiarly call the gospel, the good news of Jesus, put an end to ever again thinking of the Law as a way to gain God's favor (justification) or to become good like Him (sanctification). The central event inaugurating this new agreement was, of course, the death and resurrection of Jesus, followed by His ascension to heaven and the pouring of the Holy Spirit on all His followers at Pentecost.

What seems to be most overlooked in all the blessings brought on by the New Covenant is that it makes possible a *new way to relate.* Now, when we think someone is wrong about something, we can approach that person with an attitude entirely different from what we could muster under the old arrangement. And when a friend succeeds, perhaps where we have failed, we have the resources to be thoroughly glad for him.

A spiritual community is a New Covenant community. It is a community of people on a journey to God who relate to one another on the basis of *four provisions* of the New Covenant. To lay a foundation for discussing how spiritual, New Covenant relating actually works (which I offer in Part III), let me simply summarize these four pivotal provisions.[2]

Provision #1: A New Purity

Then I will sprinkle clean water on you, and you shall be clean.
(Ezek. 36:25 NKJV)

Just as He planned to do before the world began, God has found a way to honor His justice and holiness and still forgive us for being so bad. He poured out His righteous anger on Jesus, who never sinned, so He could pour out His boundless love on people like us who couldn't do anything but sin.

On the basis of Jesus' death—when we claim that death as what we deserved—God is released to do what He did when He first created Adam and has longed to do ever since, to sing over us with delight: "These are my kids! I'm so thrilled that they're mine." (See Zeph. 3:17.)

God's style of forgiveness is so different from ours, it's hard to actually grasp it. We've never seen anything like it. We kick Him, spit on Him, and tell Him to get lost and He invites us to a banquet. Though the cesspool remains, smelling bad as ever, He *enjoys* us as if we were bubbling springs of clear water. That's the *new purity*. It's a position, a standing before Him in the courtroom that lets us walk away from the criminal's docket fully acquitted, with no record of crime and no probationary period to see how we do.

And then the judge steps out from behind the bench, puts on street clothes, and invites us to His place for coffee. We now spend time with Someone who is actually and completely pure—and we belong. We fit. We are now in a position to celebrate each other, not to judge. Only the New Covenant makes that possible and real.

Provision #2: A New Identity

One will say, "I am the LORD's"; another will call himself by the name of Jacob; another will write with his hand, "The LORD's," and name himself by the name of Israel. (Isa. 44:5 NKJV)

People in Christ, whether they struggle with alcohol, gossip, or conceit (we all struggle with something awful), are no longer properly called sinners. We still sin, of course, but that doesn't mean we aren't saints. It would be entirely accurate to say, "St. Larry sometimes relates terribly" or "St. Peggy can be so irritating" or "St. Freddie had an affair last week."

Our new identity is something like the government's witness protection program. We are given new passports, new social security numbers, a new name, new neighbors, even new fingerprints. We actually become a different person, still with a past, but a past that has been forgotten by God; still with the accent of the place where we were born, but we're working with a diction coach to change that.

We're not criminals posing as choir members. We're legitimate, bona fide choir members who sometimes skip practice to rob a bank. We may be disciplined by not being allowed to sing for a couple of Sundays, but we're never asked to turn in our robe.

Provision #3: A New Inclination

I will put My law in their minds, and write it on their hearts.
(Jer. 31:33 NKJV)

God's Spirit has created a place in our souls deeper than the cesspool, and He has built Himself a home there. A tabernacle in the wilderness once blazed with His glory. Now our souls radiate His presence in a dark world.

The Spirit, fully God, cannot bear to live in a place filled with the snakes of pride and the insects of selfishness, so He filled the room He lives in with *new inclinations*. Love and holiness and mercy pour out of Him and fill the room with purity. Now we *want* to do good. We still have a taste for sin, sometimes a strong one we can't seem to resist. But in the Upper Room, the prospect of holiness makes us salivate like a child looking at a freshly baked apple pie.

Under the Old Covenant, we were commanded to obey. Now the same command sounds like a mother's instruction to cut a big piece of pie and add ice cream. If we don't see things that way, if we hear the command to stay moral as a prohibition, either we're not living in our Upper Room, or it hasn't yet been created in us.

Provision #4: A New Power

> I will put My Spirit within you and cause you to walk in My statutes,
> and you will keep My judgments and do them. (Ezek. 36:27 NKJV)

God's standards haven't changed. He still insists that we stay out of adult theaters and not gossip and be concerned about the well-being of people who hurt us. It's our *desires* that have changed. Now we recognize His commands as exceptionally good ideas, like looking both ways before crossing the street.

But the urge to do things our way is still strong. So God releases His Spirit to persuade us that His ways are right, that it is a privilege to obey, and that we're better off if we do. Our new inclinations lie still until the wind of the Spirit moves them, like a breeze filling the sails and moving the boat.

Last Sunday the preacher said, "True worship changes lives." In worship, our Upper Room connects with God: The Father is adored, the Son is honored, and the Spirit blows gently on the flame of our new desires. We find ourselves not only wanting to be patient with obnoxious drivers, but actually pulling it off. And when we do, it seems eerie, like a weekend golfer driving the ball three hundred yards and wondering how it happened.

In the New Covenant, God gives us a new power, the same power that raised Jesus from the dead. Surely that power can make us patient. And it's released, the power is felt, in *community*, in community with God (what we call worship) and in a certain kind of community with others (what I am calling spiritual community).

These *four provisions* of the New Covenant correspond to the *four furnishings* of the Upper Room. Here's how:

New Covenant Provisions   Upper Room Furnishings

NEW PURITY   The PASSION to WORSHIP
                            "Look what He has done for me that
                            I could never do for myself. I'm

clean, forgiven, pure as the driven snow. To God be the glory, great things He has done."

NEW IDENTITY

The PASSION to TRUST
"I am now a solid person, no longer a ghost. Who I am survives every trauma. I may have suffered abuse, but I am not an abuse victim. I am a loved child of God who was horribly abused. I can trust the One whose name I bear. He's my Father."

NEW INCLINATION

The PASSION to GROW
"Shattered dreams, fulfilled dreams—neither is the final point. Neither defines whether I live or die. I am alive and I want to grow. Every bit of what comes my way provides me with a tailor-made opportunity to do what I am most inclined to do—enjoy God and become more like His Son."

NEW POWER

The PASSION to OBEY
"I not only want to obey, I can obey. My job is to walk in the Spirit, to make space in my heart for Him to freely move."

Now, a few more comments on the *four furnishings*. Then we'll be ready to see what we can do to develop spiritual community, to enjoy the fellowship of broken people who have found their Upper Rooms.

Furnishing #1: The Passion to Worship

I sometimes wonder if the most serious mistake we make in our churches is trying to *get* people to worship. Robert Webber puts it well when he says,

> Worship is the response of the people to God's saving initiative. The inner person [Upper Room?] receives God's acts of salvation communicated in public worship with humility and in reverence, service and devotion.[3]

The passion to worship needs an opportunity for release. The Christian longs for a chance to worship. But frenetic efforts to stir the passion produce only a shallow counterfeit. Both traditional and contemporary styles of worship provide that chance when the worship leader has nothing of himself at stake and is therefore not trying to make anything happen for his sake. We must learn to structure the opportunity to worship, to re-create the event that stirs our hearts, and then get out of the way and let the Spirit do the work of drawing us to Christ.

The lonely businessman walking out of a pornographic movie has an opportunity to worship, right then as well as next Sunday. He behaved immorally, but his sin is not charged to his account. He will not go to hell because of it. He is *pure*. He behaved immorally, but he is not an immoral man.

In the sight of God, he is righteous, a wayward son, not a disowned rebel. The pressure to do right is off. His eternal destiny, his standing with God, is not at stake. Much is at stake, but not that. If he grasps the wonder of the gift of purity, he will not make a habit of sin.

Only relaxed people worship well. And we can relax because we are forgiven. God is no longer thundering at us from the top of the mountain. Now He is whispering to us as a lover—a jealous lover to be sure, but still a lover—not a critic. Saints, people who relax in their new purity, love to worship. It's their favorite thing to do.

Furnishing #2: The Passion to Trust

A good friend took issue with how I handled a tough decision. I felt defensive and annoyed. He responded by speaking more strongly. It was not a good conversation. But something in both of us is indestructible. We are each defined by the life within us that is still there even during a heated, Lower Room exchange. Later, we were able to meet as solid people, not ghosts, as two people with an enduring identity that empowered us to move toward each other with love and respect.

Our confidence is this: The God who forgave us and now accepts us as His adopted children sovereignly controls all that happens in our lives. Nothing occurs without His permission. And everything He permits is uniquely useful in making visible our new identity. In all that happens, God is able and eager to reveal who we really are. We are sons and daughters of a Father we adore, for whose sake we are willing to suffer the loss of everything but Him. Because of our new identity, we are solid people. Jesus Christ is the same yesterday, today, and forever. Because He is now in us, we are equally stable.

That truth empowers me to trust. Sometimes that's difficult. There are times when I wonder if I've grown an inch. But with my new identity, I can count on this: Eventually I will look like a real Christian.

Ghosts change identities when their circumstances change. If they lose a job they are losers. If they are betrayed by a friend, they are wounded people. If they are excluded from a circle of friends they see themselves as nothing other than rejected.

Solid people, on the other hand, remain who they were before the storm hit. And because something deep is settled within them, they are safe to be with. They require no one to make them solid, to fill them up, and they always have something to give.

I don't believe I would ever have grasped what little I know of the passion to trust without the experience of shattered dreams. Suffering exposes idolatry, it makes clear what we are depending on for life. It also surfaces what is enduring and alive within us. I am a new creation. I have wanted at times to give up on God and give myself over to pleasure, to abandon myself to sin.[4] But I haven't. Why?

At my worst moments, I have experienced the longing to trust. He is God. He is worthy of trust. And frankly, I am terrified to cross Him. It isn't the cringing fear of the kid smoking behind the barn. It is the fear of standing on a railroad track as the train approaches. God is so much *bigger* than I am.

By nature, I am not a born truster. It took a second birth to make that true. But now I am aware of a deep desire to persevere, to not shrink back, no matter what further dreams are shattered. The passion to trust survives every trial. It may need to be stirred, like a fire that has almost died, but there is always a flame. I will become like Christ. My new identity guarantees it.

Furnishing #3: The Passion to Grow

Does anyone really *believe* what the apostle James said? Do we think it's do-able? "Consider it pure joy, my brothers, whenever you face many trials."

Tell that to the man whose wife just left him. Tell that to the mom and dad burying their five-year-old son. Tell that to your friend whose surgery went badly, who will never walk again. They will hear only if they have found their way to the Upper Room.

In the 1960s, Francis Schaeffer observed that our culture is committed to personal peace and affluence. Happy and rich, things the way we want them and enough money to live well: That's the modern dream. Since that time, nothing much has changed. Postmoderns may define peace in a more spiritual sense and may see affluence more as the freedom to be what they want to be rather than the freedom to buy what they want to buy.

But it's all Lower Room thinking. We're out for ourselves, we want to be in charge of our welfare, and we claim the right to define the personal well-being we seek. We don't like anyone telling us what to do. And people ruled by those passions can make no sense of James's words.

But Upper Room saints want to grow into Christlikeness more than they want personal peace and affluence. And they're willing to pay the necessary price. There is no other way to explain the martyrs.

Only a masochist courts suffering. But Upper Room saints learn to welcome it. They believe James. They know that every bit of suffering is perfectly suited to honor their deep desire to become really good people, solid people, like Jesus. Trials are seen as providing a unique opportunity to indulge that passion.

Furnishing #4: The Passion to Obey

One married friend confessed to me he had kissed a pretty girl in a hotel lounge during an out-of-town business trip. Another told me he watched an X-rated movie in the privacy of his hotel room.

The first friend was broken, in tears, but he was careful to state that it went no farther than a kiss. I was glad that he had held back from further sexual activity but I sensed he offered that information with more pride than gratitude. I recognized myself in the Milwaukee airport bookstore incident.

My second friend had a different attitude. There was no mention of what he didn't do (He didn't say, "I watched only one movie" or, "I didn't call for a prostitute"). I heard him express brokenness over the enormity of the sin he did commit, with no effort to minimize it. Here's what he told me:

"I was thinking of no one but myself. I defiantly pressed the button and gave myself over to illegitimate pleasure for two hours.

"And yet God didn't throw me away. Something in me has changed. I know I'm capable of doing the same thing—or worse—again. But I feel a deepened desire to be with God, to draw close to Him so I'll have the power to do what I know I really want to do. And what I really want to do is to stay moral."

We don't need to sin more to deepen our appreciation of grace. We've already done quite enough to understand our desperate need. True brokenness yields appreciation. When we appreciate Christ for the kind of Person He is and the sort of love He extends to make us lovable, we begin to realize we really do want to follow Him. We experience the Passion to Obey.

A few simple sketches will set the stage for my discussion in Part III of the power of spiritual community to change lives.

Someone has a problem and he or she is struggling.

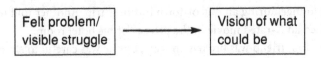

A spiritual friend sees the struggle and immediately envisions what the Spirit could do in this person's life.

That friend knows the battle is real. Beneath the problem, the Lower Room is spewing forth its poison. The snakes of *flesh dynamics* are crawling everywhere.

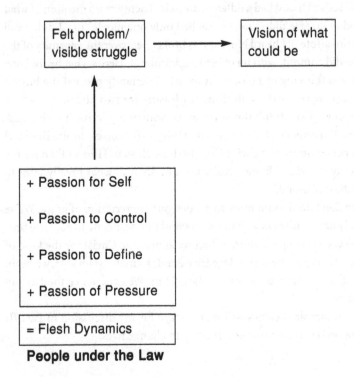

A truly spiritual friend knows that no element of someone's *Flesh Dynamics* can be improved. They can be identified, but only to be abandoned, hated, mortified, never fixed or socialized. Real change toward *Spirit Dynamics* depends on outside help, and that help has been given. There is another room, another source of energy that if released could move the individual toward the vision of what he or she could be.

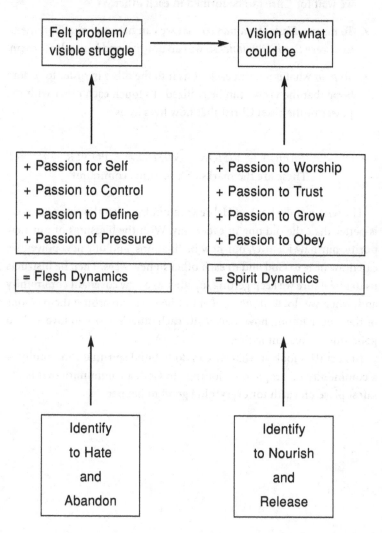

Now we can define the *tasks of spiritual community.*

- To provide a *safe place* where all that is true—both the ugly and the beautiful—can be faced.

- To *envision* what the Spirit can do, to feel the pains of childbirth as we wait for Christ to be formed in each other.

- To *discern Flesh Dynamics* so that we can hate and abandon them; to *discern Spirit Dynamics* so we can nourish and help release them.

- To *pour* what is alive in each of us into the other in order to restore hope that the vision can be realized. To touch each other with the power of the risen Christ that now lives in us.

SAFETY   VISION   WISDOM   POWER
These are the marks of a spiritual community.

The writer of the book of Hebrews reminds us that the New Covenant is better than the old one in every way. With the blessings of our new purity, our new identity, our new inclinations, and our new power, we can draw near to God and to each other in new ways. Then he instructs us to make sure we keep getting together as a new covenant community and, when we do, to *think hard* about how we can arouse the passions of the Upper Room, how we can stir each other's desire to love and do good into a consuming fire.

In Part III, I look at what we can do to build spiritual community— a community of people on a journey to God, a community that is the safest place on earth for everything good to happen.

PART III

A Way of Relating
in This World

CHAPTER 12

Turning Our Souls toward Each Other:
Three Foundational Convictions

People are longing to rediscover true community. We have had enough
of loneliness, independence, and competition.—Jean Vanier

In *Interior Castles*, Teresa of Avila writes, "This Lord of ours is so anx-
ious that we should desire Him and strive after His companionship
that He calls us constantly, time after time, to approach Him, and this
voice of His is so sweet that the poor soul is consumed with grief at being
unable to do His bidding immediately."[1]

Imagine for a moment what it would be like to spend an hour on your
knees with another Christian, weeping over your incomplete obedience
and weeping louder still, with great joy that dissolves your pride, over
the realization that the Lord still wants you. Are there really passions like
that buried deep in our hearts? Beneath our desire for things and honor
and fulfillment, is there a hunger for God?

Do we long to *worship* when life is falling apart, and to enjoy Him
as we enjoy no one and nothing else, even when life is going smoothly?
Is there a yearning to *trust* our heavenly Father when memories of our
earthly father's inconsistency, sometimes indifference, continue to
haunt us? When we think back to teenage years when we were sliding

into depression and severe eating problems and our father didn't notice, do we still experience a warm desire to trust God with everything that matters?

When life gets hard, when big things go wrong and the burdens we carry are about to crush us after having already robbed us of all joy, is it in us to still want to *grow*? Given the choice, would we actually prefer growth over relief? Would we opt for more Christlikeness over legitimate blessings that would make our lives so much happier?

When we yield to sinful urges, to the pleasures of gossip and power and revenge, when we manage our time and money with our well-being uppermost in mind, is there still a desire to *obey* that could be invigorated? Do we long to change the way we live?

Is there really an Upper Room? Is the New Covenant lovely talk? Or are its provisions hard fact? Are we pure, defined now as saints, inclined to love God and to love like God, and empowered to really change? If the things I have been talking about in Parts I and II of this book are not true, spiritual community is beyond our reach. If they are true—and I believe they are—something wonderful is possible.

A good friend fell off a ladder more than a year ago. Five hours of surgery to reconnect splintered bones in his left leg and right arm mended his leg fairly well but left his arm in bad shape. The bone extending from his shoulder to his elbow did not grow back in proper alignment.

A second surgery on that arm was recently completed. A week after surgery, the doctor reported, after studying the x-rays, "The news is not good. You'll need to wear a full cast for three months and then we'll see. I may need to go in a third time and perform even more radical surgery. At best you're a year away from any meaningful use of your arm."

Al is right-handed. He just sold his home and will move in three months. He can't even peck away at his computer, let alone carry boxes. He feels useless. But as he rode down the hospital elevator to the ground floor after hearing the grim news, the words of Paul kept coming to his mind: "If God is for us, who can be against us?" (Rom. 8:31 NKJV). In the midst of his suffering, he nearly sang. He heard the music of heaven, the voice of God, and his passion for God leaped within him.

When my friend shared the story with some of the people in his community, he could barely speak. His overwhelming emotion came from realizing God is for him, from catching a glimpse of how much that means. With bad news coming at exactly the wrong time, he found himself worshiping, trusting God, eager to grow and to continue doing good.

My passions to worship, trust, grow, and obey are unmistakably there. Other passions are there as well—my Lower Room has not yet been razed. And the good passions are often weak and hard to find, but they're there. As I spent time on my knees this morning, praying for a long list of burdens in my life and in the lives of friends, I *felt* those good passions. I do long to worship God. I desperately yearn to trust Him and to become more like Jesus and to live as He commands.

Last Sunday in church, as we sang "People Need the Lord," tears streamed down my face as I could hear my heart cry out, "I *want* the Lord." In that moment, I knew I believed that shattered dreams really are doorways to hope. The heat of joy flowed through my soul.

Community with God in worship had called out the holy passions that furnish my Upper Room. And community with Al—spiritual community as we spent time together yesterday that simply could not have happened if the Spirit were not present—further excited those same passions in both of us.

It's true that snakes from the Lower Room (I hate calling it *my* Lower Room; it's still *in* me and causes trouble but it isn't *me* anymore) still crawl about, and they sometimes bite, but their poison cannot destroy the life of Christ that's in me.

With every other Christian on earth, I am *alive.* I long to please the Father, to be like Christ, and to hear and follow the Spirit. I am involved in the life of the Trinity, impassioned by the same energy that stirs in each of them. *When those passions in me meet those same passions in you, we experience spiritual community.* And we move along, slowly but definitely, on our journey to God.

In Part III, I will lay out before you my understanding of how we can participate in that miracle, how we can be a part of spiritual community. In this chapter, I begin the discussion by thinking about three convictions that, if we do not believe them firmly and strongly, will keep us from turning our chairs completely enough for our souls to meet the souls of others.

That would be a tragedy of huge proportions, a distinctly human tragedy. We are human beings, the unique creation of a divine community of three Persons who enjoy being together more than they enjoy anything else, Persons who want to share Their joy with other people. We long to rediscover true community, to know it in our experience; we were *built* for it.

In the middle of battles with cancer, arm surgeries, divorce, and finances; in the middle of struggles against homosexuality, bulimia, self-hatred, loneliness, and depression, we yearn for intimacy. We can't help it. We can't stop it. As surely as birds were made to fly and fish to swim, we were made for community, for the kind of community the Trinity enjoys, for *spiritual* community. And to the degree we experience it, we change, we grow, we heal.

We want our small groups to mean more than they do. We want to mean more to the people in them and we want them to mean more to us. We wish that conversations with our children, young or old, with our spouses and cousins and golfing buddies and book club friends would carry us into deeper community with them, the kind of community that inflames holy passions in our souls. We often settle for congeniality, but we want more.

With legitimate covetousness that is really a Spirit-created appetite, we want our counseling sessions, whether we're counselor or counselee, to be alive with the presence of God, to be places of safety where honest souls find their way to God no matter what their background or pain.

And we want to forgive. We want to bless the persons who betrayed us, who hurt us and left us with scars that will never heal in this life. We want to pray that they find their way to God. The very fact that our hate-filled fantasies of revenge make us uncomfortable reveals that something contrary is in us; we *want* God to be glorified in that person's life.

We would give nearly anything to be part of a community that was profoundly safe, where people never gave up on one another, where wisdom about how to live emerged from conversation, where what is most alive in each of us is touched. There are three convictions that must be solidly in place if we are to make real progress in moving toward that kind of community. Let me first state them, then go back and discuss each one.

Foundational Conviction #1: Forming spiritual community is the Spirit's work. It is not ours. Our contribution is limited. Most of what we do is give up control, get out of the way, and let the Spirit take over. More than anything else, we pray.

Foundational Conviction #2: The choices we make to live in the energy of Christ, including the private choices no one can see, have a far greater impact for good on other people's lives (as bad ones have for bad) than we suspect. It is the energy that comes out of us, what we most deeply believe, that stirs passion, which nurtures or gets in the way of spiritual community. And the quality of that energy depends on our level of fellowship with God.

Foundational Conviction #3: Every bad desire is a corruption of good desire. And every good desire is a meager expression of our deepest desire: to know God. Therefore, an honest tracing of every desire, good and bad, will lead us to our Upper Room where intimacy with Him is available. Because every hunger, when followed to its source, turns out to be a hunger for God, it is vital that we live in a community safe enough for us to express and explore all our desires.

Foundational Conviction #1:
Spiritual Community Is the Work of the Spirit

Listen to Eugene Peterson:

> God the Holy Spirit conceives and forms the life of Christ in us. Our spirits are formed by Spirit—that is spiritual formation. Growth, both biological and spiritual, is a mystery, a huge mystery, intricate and complex, a work of the Holy Spirit. Most of what takes place we know very little about. Most of what goes on we can do very little about. Our part in spiritual formation is necessarily a very modest affair. We must never assume we can manage or control

it. If we try, we will most certainly be a party to deformation rather than formation.[2]

The behavioral sciences, driven by modernity's ambition, have tried to figure things out enough to control them. They have taken on the task of telling us how to relate well to each other. Training classes for small group leaders often have more to do with techniques of leadership and handling conflict and drawing quiet people into the discussion than with spiritual dependence, spiritual character, and spiritual wisdom.

In our demand that we be practical, we have nudged the Spirit aside and gone after objectives we can reach without Him. We've learned to empathize, listen well, and affirm without judging, to free people to be themselves as they define who they are and what they want. Holiness has been bumped out of the center and replaced by healthy adjustment, self-acceptance, and relief from struggle.

Peterson comments, "When spiritual formation permits itself to be dominated by behavioral sciences, it is inevitably secularized and individualized with occasional prayerful nods upwards for help in self-actualization. Narcissus on his knees."[3]

In all my years as a therapist, I think I've learned one lesson more than any other. It is the lesson of patience. My lack of humility has kept me from learning it better, but the reality of people's lives, including mine, has forced me to wait for God to work.

Ten uneventful sessions may be followed by a supernatural moment in the eleventh where everything changes. My counselee improves. Substantial integration of multiple personalities sometimes occurs quickly after months of no discernible progress. Without the Spirit and the Christ He represents, I can do nothing of real value. That's a lesson I must learn if I am to participate in spiritual community. It's a lesson only God can teach me.

When the Israelites were preparing to enter Canaan, God told them they would drive out their enemies "little by little" (Exod. 23:30). Growth would be slow. But in another place He said, "You will drive them out and annihilate them quickly" (Deut. 9:3).

The contradiction disappears when we see that the enemies referred to in the two passages are different. *Lesser* enemies, the Jebusites, Hivites, and others, would be conquered slowly. The more fearsome enemy, the giants that made the faithless spies tremble, would be driven out quickly.

But that introduces a new problem. Are we to learn that we will get over small problems slowly, but big problems will take no time at all to handle? That makes no sense, until we see what happened when Israel invaded the land.

The book of Joshua lets us know that Israel took on the lesser enemy first and spent *seven years* driving them out. At the end of that slow conquest, Caleb asks permission to go after the giants, and he destroys them in a day.

Perhaps the lesson is this: God intends for us to depend entirely on Him for every victory. After we struggle for years against small problems that pride tells us should be easily disposed, He supplies the power to conquer big problems quickly.

I'm sitting in a glass-enclosed porch as I write, within easy earshot but not so easy reach of the phone. For the last ten minutes, both lines have been ringing. My wife is home. I thought she would answer them. After all, I am under deadline pressures to write this book. With a burst of Lower Room energy, I just stormed out of my hallowed writing sanctuary to quiet the jangling phone and to see what was occupying my wife.

She informed me the rascal we are dog-sitting just escaped from her pen and a project she is managing just hit a snag. She is temporarily experiencing a burst of frenzy. As she put both hands to her head as if to pull out her hair (her response to my innocent question, "Didn't you hear the phone?"), I could feel the words forming in my throat: "I've got to get some writing done today."

Instead, remembering what I've said about the Spirit creating better urges in an alleged Upper Room, I looked at her and kindly said, "You're handling a lot right now." When I listened to my heart, I realized that's what I *wanted* to say. She smiled, not broadly, but I saw it.

One small battle won. Maybe in seven more years, the Spirit's life will pour out of me like water from a geyser.

Our most difficult work in forming spiritual community is to stop working so hard. "In repentance and rest is your salvation, in quietness and trust is your strength, but you would have none of it" (Isa. 30:15 NIV).

If you want to prepare for involvement in spiritual community, acknowledge that no amount of knowledge and skill and effort will make it happen, no more than a short person can will himself to be taller. Growth, both within us individually and in our relationships, is a mysterious work of the Spirit.

No training program, whether premarital counseling or small group leadership meetings or a series of classes for lay counselors in the church, will adequately equip anyone to develop spiritual community. Training has its place, but prayer is more the point. Humility *demands* prayer. Brokenness, the heartfelt admission that without Christ we can do nothing, *enjoys* prayer.

Foundational Conviction #2:
We Best Promote Another's Holiness by Pursuing Our Own. Our Private Choices Affect the Kind of Influence We Have on People

Pascal once wrote, "The slightest movement affects the whole of nature; one stone can alter the whole sea. Likewise, in the realm of grace, the slightest action affects everything because of its consequences; therefore everything matters."[4]

Peter Kreeft's comments on that thought from Pascal take it to an uncomfortable conclusion, alive with frightening and wonderful possibilities. He suggests that when someone says a loving word to another, "some martyr three thousand miles and three hundred years away may receive enough grace to endure his trials because of you. And if you sin one more time this afternoon, that martyr may weaken, compromise, and be broken."[5]

I wonder if my decision to speak from my Upper Room to my wife a moment ago will somehow strengthen a member of the body of Christ. It requires only a little stretch to believe that my friend's decision to not watch an adult movie in his hotel room two weeks ago might help his daughter enter marriage as a virgin.

Preparation to become part of spiritual community not only includes the prayer of brokenness, "Lord, without You I can do nothing," but also the indulgence of holy appetites, "Lord, I long to bless my wife, my daughter, my friend. Therefore, I will value holiness above either pleasure or relief from pain or the illegitimate satisfaction that sin, like barking at my wife, so easily brings."

Foundational Conviction #3:
A Safe Place to Own and Trace Our Desires to Their Source
Will Put Us in Touch with Our Hunger for God

Never was the psalmist more aware of his soul than when he said:

> *One thing I ask of the LORD,*
> *this is what I seek:*
> *that I may dwell in the house of the LORD*
> *all the days of my life,*
> *to gaze upon the beauty of the LORD*
> *and to seek Him in his temple. (Ps. 27:4 NIV)*

We are told to "above all else, guard your heart, for it is the wellspring of life" (Prov. 4:23 NIV). The heart is the exact center of our personality, it is the seat of desire, "the meeting place between people and God."[6] We are a generation that has lost touch with our heart. The distractions of busyness have sealed us off from what we most desire. We keep ourselves distracted in fear that we might discover desires that no one will satisfy.

I spoke with a loving, godly woman who described her rape: "It took something from me. I am no longer sure of my femininity. My deepest desires as a woman now seem like my enemy. I am afraid to embrace how deeply I want to be safe, to be treated tenderly." She loves, but she holds back. A moat surrounds her soul. She has filled it with the alligators of distraction.

Addictions are the expression of distracted desire. We become enslaved to immediate and consuming satisfaction because we're afraid to own what we most deeply want. Longing for what will never come is torture, and torture demands relief. *Addictions* end the pain, at least for a while. And *distractions* keep us from facing the desires that addictive behavior cannot touch. I agree so deeply with James Houston when he says, "The unsatisfied longing for God is what drives human beings above all else."[7]

Terror grips us when we begin to sense how badly we want to be liked, respected, appreciated, how jealous we are of others who are more liked than we are, or at least more noticed. Rather than following the path of desire to its source, we feel too ashamed and hide our desires from view, even our own.

We need a safe place to admit and explore our desires, a community of fellow journeyers who believe that our desires are not at root shameful but thoroughly human and already met in Jesus. I don't know if many of us can imagine a group of people, even a small group, where we would feel safe enough to meaningfully explore who we are with confidence so that the end point would be a joyful meeting with God.

Perhaps if we once see that beneath every desire is a yearning for God, we will do a better job of providing the safety of hope. Perhaps then we will realize that our desires are not to be laughed at, derided, or put away, but to be traced to their source and given full expression.

We have covered three convictions to begin our search for spiritual community: Ponder them, discuss them in your group and with your friends, study the Scriptures to see if they have biblical support. Then move on, not leaving those convictions behind, but building on them an approach to developing spiritual community.

CHAPTER 13

The Fork in the Road to
Spiritual Community

He [the mystic] is quietly, deeply, and sometimes ecstatically aware of
the presence of God in his own nature.—A. W. Tozer

My schedule has been full. I flew in last night from Boston, three days
earlier from Quebec City. Tomorrow morning I leave for Dallas.
I must be feeling the pressure. Twice this past week I have exploded with
frustration over trivial matters that deserved only a "Doggone it! Oh, well."

It's been a good season these past few months; active, pinched for time,
plagued by endless responsibilities, but still good. I have sensed the Spirit
moving in me personally and through me in recent ministry opportunities and conversations. I've felt important, I think in a holy way, to a
few people. God is using me to stir some of His children to love Him
and trust Him a little more. That produces joy. And I've been similarly
stirred by others.

Why then, this morning, do I feel so isolated, so heavy, as if something had died?

For several months now, a keen sense of fellowship with Christ and
a fierce awareness of mission that, although intense, has felt peaceful,

have combined to keep discouragement at bay. But last night, when the wheels of the 757 hit the Denver runway, a tired feeling of defeat swept through me.

Lower Room energy took over. I didn't want to pray. I craved a sausage pizza and, as I walked through the terminal, I felt angrily drawn to Mrs. Field's cookie shop. I walked by, but only with ill-humored self-control. My spiritual state plummeted.

I arrived home to an empty house. Rachael is away with friends for three days. My feeling of isolation deepened.

I rose early this morning to pray, read, meditate, and celebrate the Lord's Supper. I didn't *want* to, I felt no pleasure at the prospect, but I knew I was in a bad way. I felt vulnerable to the enemy.

In my journal I wrote these words: "A new battle is raging again. I don't know how to fight it." Then I paused. I put my pen down, stared at the bread and wine sitting on the fireplace hearth, then, with an odd presentiment, wrote, "Maybe I do."

There was another pause, this one perhaps two minutes. Then this sentence flowed from my pen: "Do I need to speak with a friend, a spiritual friend, to confess my sins, swallow my shame, and humble myself to receive strength from him?"

One friend quickly came to mind—the same one I had yelled at in Chicago a year ago. I had just been with him three days earlier. In an instant, I decided to call him. That decision created immediate hope. I *knew* what presenting my burden would arouse in him. And I knew it was precisely what I wanted.

He would, of course, feel concern. But I didn't expect the usual dose of empathy given by so many—empathy that easily turns maudlin. I knew I would sense his *delight* in me. Nothing I could say, no struggle I might reveal, would disgust him or make him turn his chair away. This man *believes* in me. I knew that wouldn't change.

The battle being fought within me would not discourage him or cause him to worry that I might be going down for the third time. He would stay calm. He would not feel desperate, but rather hopeful, even excited, knowing that every battle is a sign of life and the outcome is already settled: Yes, I would live.

Stirred by his heart, this man's mind would spot the Spirit working in the middle of the mess and, although he might not say it, he would also notice evidence of Flesh Dynamics. He knows I have a Lower Room. And he might point out what's there. But he likes talking about my Upper Room more.

He would also attend to his own spirit. He would trust the Holy Spirit to move in him, and he would, I knew, offer whatever was provoked.

I just called him. He is in a meeting. He'll call back as soon as it's through. As I sit, staring at the fire and the still-unconsumed bread and wine, I sense that I am being lifted to my Upper Room, carried there by the sheer force of the godly passions I know are in this man, passions I will soon experience because I have chosen to put myself where I will feel them. I have turned my chair, this time to *receive*.

My friend will *celebrate* Christ in me, he will not judge me, and I will feel safe. He will *envision* the reality of my new identity as it is and will become. He will *discern* the Spirit and flesh competing for control; and he will *pour out* what is most supernaturally natural in him. What he says will matter. The energy carrying his words will matter more. It will be the energy of Christ. Right now, this man is for me the safest place on earth. Community with him has become a means of grace, an opportunity to experience the source of true safety.

Spiritual community can be thought of as an exchange between two or more people that reflects those four passions: *the safety of celebration, the hope of vision, the wisdom of loving discernment,* and *the power of touch.*

He just called back. I told him I was in a spiritual battle and described it to him, with tears. Here's a condensed version of what might seem a rather ordinary conversation.

Friend: "You aren't surprised by all this, are you?"
Larry: "Well, no. I know I have a Lower Room."
Friend: "The fact that you're so bothered by losing fellowship with Christ really encourages me. You really want Him."

I felt celebrated, safe, enjoyed. His words stirred me to worship. Beneath it all, I *am* pure.

Friend: "You're so far ahead of me. When I get discouraged, I stay
there. But you're wrestling with God and calling me."

I felt envisioned. He seemed to recognize something solid in me; my
passion to trust roused itself and I relaxed a bit.

Friend: "What made you so troubled by your struggles? I would
think you'd be used to them by now."

I went on to explain how excited I feel to be fighting my own battle
well, knowing it might help my wife and sons and friends to fight their
battles well, too. As I spoke, I realized I had been seen in the Upper Room.
I was speaking with the passion to grow, to keep in step with the Spirit,
and I knew He was working.

Friend: "Do you think it's important to call a friend like you just
did? Why wouldn't you just wrestle with God privately? I'm glad
you called, but I don't know what I add."

Those questions were what occurred to him as we talked. They weren't
especially clever, but they were somehow powerful. I felt energized to
respond with Upper Room passion.

Larry: "It was really a simple choice. God *told* me to call. I could
obey or not. Maybe we don't take seriously enough that we are
Christ's body. Maybe that's more than a metaphor. You're
actually presenting Christ to me, and I think He wants to feed us
through each other. If we're locked in a Tibetan prison and can't
talk to anyone, then He'll find a more direct way to give us what
we need. But if community is available, maybe that's the
restaurant where we need to eat a meal."
Friend: "There's really more to being together than we think, isn't
there. It's mysterious, even mystical."

As he offered me what was burning in him—curiosity, an awareness
of transcendence, the awe of entering mystery—I was thrilled that I had

obeyed God by calling my friend. I hung up the phone, stood up, and shouted, "Yes!" I sat down again, and took the bread and wine with gusto.

I'm broken, but I'm alive. The blood of the New Covenant has made me pure, given me a new identity, created an appetite for God stronger than all other appetites, and empowered me with His Spirit that sometimes touches me through my spiritual community.

Am I discouraged? Not a bit. I am filled with joy unspeakable and full of glory. The Son told the Father He gave the glory to me. And He did. The glory of divine life is in me. The Spirit just used a friend to stir it up.

This encounter serves as a lesson for me about how to stimulate others toward love and good deeds. Spiritual community, as C. S. Lewis once said, is a good laboratory for discovering God.

The Christian therapeutic culture assumes it is strengthening Lewis's thought when it thinks of community as a place to build up self-esteem. In fact, it is taking us in an altogether different direction. I do not want to be heard as suggesting that these four elements of spiritual community—celebrating, envisioning, discerning, touching—are ways to merely give us good feelings about ourselves. I did not leave that conversation with my friend more aware of my worth. I left it more aware of God's.

Self-esteem—what the therapeutic culture often means by that term and what it assumes is necessary for emotional health—is more a hearty weed to be pulled out of the human personality than a fragile flower to nourish. Our strategies to preserve and enhance the *self* reflect the godless energy of people who are determined, at all cost, to find themselves, without yielding center stage to Christ.

It cannot be done. The effort should not be encouraged. When holy passions come out of one person into another, the effect is not to make us more convinced merely of our own value. It is to honor the reality of Christ in us and all He has done that no one else could ever do.

Spiritual community first celebrates God, and people secondarily as marvelous opportunities to display God's grace. It envisions how the Spirit could further reveal the character of Christ through us. It excitedly discerns evidence of the Spirit at work and gently but relentlessly exposes flesh-driven maneuvering. It pours the actual life of Christ into souls, for without that life souls are utterly dead and devoid of value.

As a people, we may be ready to recognize that violence, whether blatant when two teenage boys shoot their schoolmates in a Colorado high school, or subtle when folks like us speak with the intent to control or hurt or exploit a fellow image bearer, is more the result of offended flesh-driven egotism than of desperate yearnings for love. Brokenness and humility must be the context for feeling how badly we want to be loved. Without that context, we decide that being loved is our right and that denial of our rights is legitimate cause for revenge.

When I called my friend, the passions that flowed out of him into me did not satisfy a demand. They rather awakened the grateful realization that I am loved. They did not enhance self-esteem, they deepened worship and they helped me experience my God-given value. When my needs and my feelings and my self are the indulged center of things, all hell will eventually break loose. When Christ is preeminent in me and in my friend, the kingdom of heaven arrives on earth.

The church is a community of people on a journey to God.

The community is spiritual if the passions aroused in us, as we meet with each other, are the direct and supernatural effect of living in the reality of what God has provided in the New Covenant. Let me explain.

The Passion to Celebrate

In our Lower Room, we are passionate for *self*. We don't worship God; we try to use Him, then angrily dismiss Him when He proves unhelpful. That's sin. The New Covenant provides forgiveness, total and complete. We're given a *new purity*. When we even feebly grasp the radical nature of our new position as once filthy people now absolutely clean, an Upper Room passion to worship develops.

As we live in a community of forgiven people, the provision of purity frees spiritual friends to fundamentally delight in each other no matter what is going on in our lives. There may be reason for rebuke, discipline, even hard words, but in spiritual community the spirit of celebration is never lost.

The passion to worship God for His gift of radical forgiveness and unblemished purity translates into the passion to celebrate when we look at each other.

Not many people feel celebrated. At the root of what we call psychological disorder is the opposite of feeling celebrated: feeling unwanted, despised, the project of people who will discard us if we don't turn out as they want. A relationship that offers celebration heals the soul by releasing the passion to worship in the one who is celebrated and knows why. There is no safer place to connect to our own sin and shame than in a community that celebrates the gift of purity—a gift that nothing can soil. In that spiritual community, people have no secrets.

The Passion to Envision

Perhaps the dominant passion in our Lower Rooms is the determination to manage life with resources we can manage: the passion to control. We don't trust God, we've concluded prayer is a waste of time, so we take on the job of arranging for our own happiness.

In what was billed as comedy, George Carlin complained that the odds in prayer are fifty-fifty, so why bother? That leaves us alone and terrified, confident that no one cares about our well-being as fully as we do, and trusting only ourselves. When our resources run dry, we lapse into emotional disorder, a way of begging the world to do for us what it's never done, and at the same time keeping a safe distance from it. That's sin.

First, Jesus forgives us. Then, through the New Covenant He provides a *new identity*, a kind of down payment guaranteeing that God is indeed worthy of trust. With our new identity in place, we begin to realize that nothing can interfere with Christ's purpose to make us like Himself. We're given His name, we're Christ-ones; then, slowly, the Spirit develops His character in us through every circumstance of life. The passion to *trust* begins to stir, nudging aside the passion to *control*. We relax, we rest, we get quiet, we stop working so hard.

When we're together in a community of people with a new identity, we move toward them with confidence that they, too, are on a journey led by a sure Guide. Patience is, of course, required: Pornographers buy another magazine, alcoholics take another drink, gossips still gossip and complainers still complain. But we no longer label them as pornographers, alcoholics, gossips, or complainers. Now, we view each other as saints, each with his or her own set of problems, but still saints. Spiritual friends treat each other with dignity and respect. They envision what one day will be, fully in heaven, substantially in this life.

The passion to trust that stirs in each saint, kindled by the provision of a New Identity, translates into the passion to envision what the other is becoming as we journey together.

There is a difference between seeing someone as your project and having a vision for how the Spirit is shaping their new identity. In the first, the energy is self-oriented: I want you to become this for *me*. In the second, the passion is love for God and the other: I want you to become more like God so He will be clearly revealed to people who know you, and so you will be happy.

The Passion to Discern

Lower Room dwellers wrongly define life and death. Whatever has caused pain is defined as death, something at all costs to avoid. Whatever has brought pleasure is understood to be life, and is therefore pursued. The passion coming from the Lower Room is to feel good quickly, to manipulate life's circumstances to maximize our experience of pleasure and minimize the pain: to live and not die. That's foolishness.

Suffering becomes an enemy and the One who allows it becomes the greater enemy. Therefore God is hated in suffering. Still He forgives us. And through the New Covenant, the Spirit creates in us a new appetite, a new set of inclinations, a *new disposition*. Before, we had taste buds only for self-actualization, self-fulfillment. Now we actually prefer holiness. We'd rather love like God than enjoy the devil's pleasures.

Now life is defined as knowing God and making Him known by becoming like His Son. That provision brings along with it a new passion. When life gets hard, certainly we'd prefer to smooth out the bumps and, if we can, we do. And of course we like to feel good about ourselves. But our deeper passion is to *grow*, to change, to mature, and to have the Spirit more completely form the life of Christ in us.

We welcome trials as a means of spiritually forming us. When we suffer or when life is pleasant, the New Covenant provision of a new disposition releases the passion to grow. When we get together with other similarly disposed friends, we turn into excited miners looking for gold. We know the new disposition is there in the other person—God has said it is and we've seen it in ourselves—so we correct our vision till we find it. It may take some digging, but that's what miners do when they know there's gold beneath the rock.

The passion to grow aroused by our new disposition translates into a passion to see into others, to sensitively discern the energy of both their rooms, to feel excitement when the gold of Upper Room urges is discovered and to expose as worthless the fool's gold of the Lower Room.

When spiritual friends share their stories, the others listen without working. They rest. There's nothing to fix, nothing to improve. A spiritual community feels undisturbed quiet as they listen, certainly burdened, sometimes to the point of anguish for what others must endure, but still resting in the knowledge that the life within, the passion for holiness, is indestructible. It needs only to be nourished and released.

The Passion to Empower

When we live in our Lower Room, we feel pressure. We *know* we should do better, but we just can't. And we wonder why others, especially God, aren't more sensitive to our pain. We're pressured, defiant, and self-pitying. We hate the Law as God has given it, so we reduce it to standards we can keep, then congratulate ourselves for being pretty good people, considering what we've been through.

I heard an angry wife say, "I know I shouldn't be so angry, but he really ought to be grateful I haven't killed him." She meant it.

That's sin. In the New Covenant, along with the ever-present forgiveness, we're provided with a *new power*. We *want* to worship, to trust, and to grow, and when it's clear that we should do this and not that, God Himself supplies the power to make it possible. We're empowered to obey. We begin to experience a *passion to obey*.

In its most mature form, obedience is a matter of relating well, of giving to others what is best for them without any thought of the price it requires of us. When we spend time together with spiritual friends indwelt by the same power, we experience a deep desire to be an instrument of God, to inflame the passion to obey in others.

The passion to obey, excited by the Holy Spirit who is our new power, translates into a passion to give whatever the Spirit rouses in us to others so that they will be further stirred to obey our Lord.

We actually present Christ to each other when we freely offer whatever is most spiritually alive within us. The result is movement toward holiness, in both parties.

Spiritual community heals the soul. It does so by releasing into someone else passions that lift that person into the Upper Room. From there, Lower Room passions are exposed as contingent on a lie. That lie is the whopper that God is not the Supreme Satisfier of souls, that He is not infinitely good and worthy to be radically trusted.

Lower Room passions are not rearranged, reinterpreted, or redirected. They are discarded as the pathetic boasts of a bully who has no courage, no muscles, who can never win. But they must be seen as such before we will disregard them. Only seeing better passions that are solid and noble, that fit the shape of our human souls, frees us to recognize evil passions for what they are.

Let's review an earlier sketch.

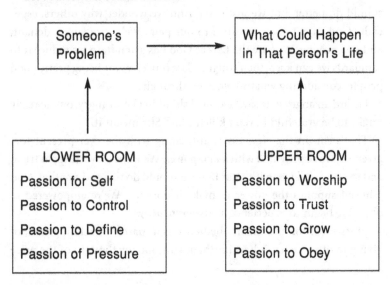

The only way to deal with people's problems is to weaken the grip Lower Room passions have on them. But the passions themselves cannot be weakened. They can only be experienced as weaker when Upper Room passions are aroused and fanned into a bonfire. That is precisely what happens when a community of people, ruled by their own Upper Room passions, offers an individual a relationship that forcefully communicates four messages:

1. *We accept you*—we celebrate your purity in Christ, as we worship God.

2. *We believe in you*—we envision your identity in Christ and what you can become as we trust God.

3. *We see you and are glad to stay involved*—we discern your good passions and delight in them; we discern your bad passions and know they do not define you, as we ourselves continue to grow in Christ.

4. *We give to you*—we apply no pressure to change you. The power to change is already in you. We give you what is most alive in us with the prayer that it will set you free to indulge your deepest desires, as we eagerly obey God.

Perhaps a sketch will present my ideas in clearer form.

When a person with a problem turns his chair toward spiritual community, this is what that community sees.

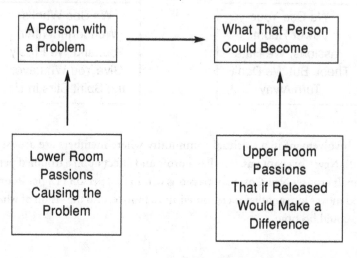

When spiritual community sees a troubled person, New Covenant passions *toward God* are translated into New Covenant passions *toward that person.*

New Covenant Provision	Passionate Response to God	Passionate Response to Person
1. New Purity	Worship	Celebration
2. New Identity	Trust	Envisioning
3. New Disposition	Eagerness to Grow	Discernment
4. New Power	Eagerness to Obey	Giving

As chairs are turned, this is what the troubled person hears from spiritual community and receives as food for his soul.

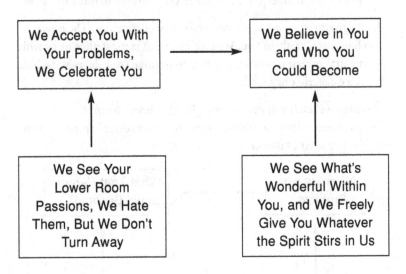

Involvement in a spiritual community where members are aroused with New Covenant passions has a profound effect upon a troubled person. It arouses New Covenant passions within that person's Upper Room and moves him another inch, sometimes a foot, toward the vision of what he could become.

But so much depends on whether the community is spiritual. Do we respond to the troubled person with New Covenant passions? Do we *experience* the movement of the Spirit in our own hearts? Are we aroused with the passions Christ feels as He looks at the troubled person?

Do we *celebrate* our spouses when they hurt us?

Do we joyfully *envision* what our shiftless and irresponsible and cynical and spiritually shallow son could become? Do we yield that child to the Trinity's care, recognizing our impotence to make anything good happen with our own maneuvering?

When we talk with a discouraged or morally compromised friend, do we *discern* traces, sometimes no larger than a speck of dust on a well-vacuumed carpet, of the Spirit's movement, and can we see the real battle raging in the Lower Room?

Do we recognize the Spirit's movement in our hearts and freely *give,* pouring whatever life is in us into the heart of an irritating colleague?

Managers, people who stop with head knowledge of the gospel and continue to manage their lives with their own resources, never experience those passions. Only mystics do.

The road to spiritual community has now reached a fork. We must go one way or another, and we have come to see that we can no longer walk the management path. It doesn't work. It quenches the Spirit and leaves us handling conflicted community with congeniality, cooperation, consolation, counseling, or conformity.

Yet there is no greater determination in our fallen hearts than to manage things. We long to reduce mystery to manageable categories. To turn for help to experts who can figure out what's wrong with us and apply the appropriate remedy. To come up with a system to follow that does not require profound spiritual depth.

This fork in the road presents the broad path of continuing on as *managers,* of trying to develop healing communities while we remain in the Lower Room. It also presents the narrow path of becoming *mystics,* not the anti-rational, experience-dependent dreamers that are perversions of mysticism, but the people that Tozer describes:

The word "mystic" refers to that personal spiritual experience common to the saints of Bible times and well known to multitudes of persons in the post-Biblical era. I refer to the evangelical mystic who has been brought by the gospel into intimate fellowship with the Godhead. His theology is no less and no more than is taught in the Christian Scriptures. He differs from the ordinary orthodox Christian only because he experiences his faith down in the depths of his sentient being while the other does not. He is quietly, deeply, and sometimes almost ecstatically aware of the Presence of God in his own nature and in the world around him. His religious experience is something elemental, as old as time and the creation. It is immediate acquaintance with God by union with the Eternal Son. It is to know that which passes knowledge.[1]

A mystic, by that definition, is a spiritual person, someone who knows, in the Hebrew sense, the person of God. A mystic experiences the presence and the movement of God within his soul. Spiritual passions are aroused. He has learned to sit in the Upper Room quietly enough to actually experience God.

Managers never contribute to spiritual community. They never connect. Only mystics do.

The rest of the book suggests what is required to choose the path of mysticism, and what can pour out of us into others that creates spiritual community.

CHAPTER 14

Managers or Mystics:
The Mystery of Community

The best is perhaps what we understand least.—C. S. Lewis

Christians are meant to be "spiritual" in the sense that they
are meant to be "led by the Spirit" and to "live by the Spirit."
—Simon Tugwell

We're really out of our element as we talk of spiritual community. And that's as it should be.What does a father say to his daughter when she breaks curfew for the tenth time? Parenting experts seem to know, but parents are never sure. Community, we must freely admit, is amystery. It cannot be reduced to principles or boxed in by rules and regulations.

What defines spiritual community are the passions aroused in its members when they get together; and passions are not easily managed. A close friend told me after a long conversation with a son facing hard times, "Our emotions were all over the place." I know what she means.

It is still tempting to try to manage community because it matters so much. We don't want to trust Someone else to get it right. We work at our marriages by carefully following principles of communication and strategies for conflict resolution. Counselors have carved out a profession for themselves by developing theories of what's wrong with people and coming up with procedures for reversing the disorder.

But soul care and all relationships are *spiritual* activity. Good relating that stirs life in another, whether in counseling, family, or friendship, depends on the Spirit and cannot, therefore, be managed, because He cannot be managed.

What we have come to at this point in the book is this: *A safe community where souls can rest, love, and heal is a community where people look at one another and are stirred by the Spirit to experience holy passions. Out of those passions they speak.*

How do we manage that? We don't. We become mystics. We put ourselves in the humble position of dependence and let God do it.

But what does that mean? There still is something for us to do. What is it? As I use the term, mysticism involves *neither* an emphasis on experience that minimizes the essential value of thought-through, rationally presented truth *nor* a special interior intensity reserved only for the more ethereal, less practical, and strange saints among us. A plumber fixing toilets and a monk at prayer can equally be mystics.

Perhaps an attempt at definition will help: *Mysticism is the felt arousal of spiritual passions within the regenerate heart, passions that can have no existence apart from a Spirit-revealed knowledge of truth and the promptings of the same Spirit to enjoy that truth.*

The difficulty, of course, is that we're either managers or bad mystics. We tend to feel all the wrong passions. Two days ago, a friend offered a comment that stung. It seemed to me that he intended to demean me, to pay me back for an earlier offense I had committed against him. My apology had apparently not settled the matter. The best question for me to ask of myself was also the most painful one: What passions were aroused in me as I listened to his cutting remark?

Was I concerned for self? Did I feel the weariness of relationships never quite working as they should and focus on that weariness? Did I wonder if I was a bit paranoid to interpret his words as demeaning?

Was I determined to stay in control? Did I ask where I had failed this man and what I could do to win back his kindness? Did I feel annoyed and look for some way to get the upper hand? "Maybe he doesn't know his impact. I'll let him know he's hurt me."

Was I preoccupied with feeling better about myself, with recovering a sense of immediately felt life? Did I quickly move to get another cup of coffee and pick up a cookie on the way? (We were at a buffet restaurant.) Was it a coincidence that I instantly thought of Chuck sitting across the way, a man who always compliments me, and felt an urge to chat with him? Did I look for some way to write off my offending friend as jealous, insecure, or arrogant so I could consider the source of the comment and not feel quite so stung?

Was I pressured to handle the moment well? Did my mind jump to a Bible verse I should obey, perhaps the one about a soft answer turning away wrath? Did I feel down on myself for my quick flash of anger and did I start trying to figure out what's wrong with me that I could work on?

I suppose every one of the above passions rose within me. I should expect it. They all come from my Lower Room, from that place where I intend to handle whatever happens. They are the passions of a *manager* and they lead only to strengthened efforts to manage well. If they are the only passions rising in me, the conversation with my friend, no matter how apparently gracious or blatantly nasty, will never leave the basement. My Diabolical Self will be released.

A shift is in order, a radical shift that most of us rarely consider. We must shift from management to mysticism, from operating as managers in that tense moment to living as mystics. Only then will Upper Room passions be aroused. Only then will we experience ourselves as solid people, wounded perhaps and hurting, struggling with resentment and insecurity, but actually aware of an urge to celebrate this person as a pure saint, to envision what he could become, to see evidence of the Spirit in the midst of his petulance. Only then will we want to bless him.

Until that shift happens, spiritual community will not occur. Everything will be natural, no different from if the Old Covenant were still in effect. The proper response is not simply to try hard to do better. That response continues the problem.

The road to becoming a Spirit-led mystic begins with seeing the Cross as our opportunity to relate with God, intimately, passionately, enjoyably. The starting point for spiritual community is not learning and practicing relational skills. It is relating with God, drawing near to Him through the door opened by the New Covenant. It is realizing that the doctrine of the New Covenant is an invitation to something far more exciting and satisfying than an erotic evening.

Listen to F. W. Faber express poetically his experience of the Holy Spirit:

> Ocean, wide-flowing Ocean, Thou,
> Of uncreated love;
> I tremble as within my soul
> I feel Thy waters move.
>
> Thou art a sea without a shore;
> Awful, immense Thou art;
> A sea which can contract itself
> Within my narrow heart.[1]

Orthodoxy that is cold is only academically orthodox. It stimulates the Lower Room passion to manage:

- "The Bible says this. What shall I do?"
- "I want to love my husband well. What does that mean?"
- "My children are a heritage from the Lord. I *will* train them properly."

That passion produces *scholars* with no higher ambition than to precisely articulate truth. It produces *moralists* who want only to bring their lives and the lives of others into behavioral conformity with biblical standards. It produces *counselors* who train to understand what's wrong with people and to technically intervene.

Until we recover the biblical idea of heart, until we get in touch with the Eternal Community's creation of our inmost being that yearns to connect with a perfectly loving person, we will remain rationalists, managers, orthodox in doctrine, perhaps, but stirred primarily to control. We will never learn the humility of giving up power over others. We will never realize that any power we have over another can stir only Lower Room passions.

"Pascal condemned the cold logic of his contemporary Descartes as only fit for a 'geometric man,' because spiritual realities cannot be described by mathematical theorems."[2]

With the eyes of our heart, we must see spiritual truth as reality that goes beyond reason, as reality with a beauty that exceeds the symmetry of order and the grandeur of vastness. Final reality is personal, it is three-persons-in community. Managers try to explain it and call themselves theologians. Mystics enjoy it and become lovers.

When God first created people, He placed them in a garden, the biblical symbol of God's presence "where He is loved and desired above all else."[3] And He named the garden Eden, a word that means delight in the sense of erotic rapture.

When I ponder the significance of God placing Adam and Eve in the Garden of Eden and not in a university library or a business board room, something stirs in me. I begin to realize pornography is a closer substitute for God than a prosperous profit statement; that sexual pleasure is a picture of our ecstatic union with God. Likewise, when we ignore God, sexual pleasure becomes our tyrant.

Let me say it clearly: *Spiritual passion for God is meant to exceed the consuming pleasure of sexual release.* To settle for less dishonors God. It is like a woman reciting romantic poetry on her wedding night and never climbing into bed. It misses the point.

The spirituality of a community can be measured not merely by its doctrinal statement but by the passions that are most deeply aroused. Is our passion for worship elbowing out our passion for self? Does our passion to trust nudge aside our passion to control? Does our passion to grow make us willing to suffer whatever pain is needed? Is our passion to obey relieving the pressure to do something right? Instead, is it causing us to delight with anything we do right?

Spiritual passions, those generated by realizing the staggering provisions of the New Covenant, are the centerpiece of spiritual community. They are what we pour into one another. Truly spiritual passions communicate more truth to deeper places in people than well-presented teaching, because they can exist only if the gospel is true.

Forgive me for reporting a compliment I received two evenings ago. I finished my spring lectures that night and two students said to me: "You seem so much more inviting these last few weeks than earlier. It made what you were saying so much more important for us to hear. Your teaching stirred us, but your way of teaching stirred us more."

Here is perhaps the pivotal key to mysticism: *When spiritual people interact, something pours out of one soul and into another soul as surely and literally as life-giving fluid flows out of a man's body and into a woman's body during sexual intercourse.*

Modernists, and far too many Christians, are afraid of mystery. A good friend whom I count as a mentor, Selwyn Hughes from England, many years ago listened to me teach for a week. Afterward he said, "I think you're afraid of the Holy Spirit. I counted seven times when something you said visibly stirred people. As soon as that happened, each time, you said something funny. Larry, notice your delight when the Spirit pours out of you into others. Let yourself enjoy it."

We naturally fear what we cannot control. Losing control destroys something in us, something that needs to be killed: pride.

When we approach relationship as managers, we soon become bored. What we can manage is not worth having. Even Freud, the father of rationalism in therapy, once wrote to his fiancée before an impending visit, "When you come to me, little princess, come to me with an irrational love." He wanted more than what his mind could explain and manage. At heart, he was a mystic. We all are.

Pascal put it this way: "If we submit everything to reason, our religion will be left with nothing mysterious or supernatural."[4]

It might be a profitable and humbling exercise to pay attention to whatever passions stir in us during our times with people, perhaps our marital arguments or even our marital pleasures, conversations in our small group, lunchtime chats with a friend, or counseling sessions. Record them in your journal. Discuss them with one good friend.

We will likely be discouraged. Snakes from the Lower Room are crawling everywhere.

- *How do I get through to her? She is so stubborn.*

- *I can't believe he said that. What an idiot.*

- *Did I say something stupid? I'd better keep my mouth shut.*

- *What on earth is going on with my client? I've got to figure it out.*

It could be different. With the New Covenant in place, we could be stirred by better passions. As we become obsessed with a Person who makes filthy people clean by becoming filthy Himself, who then claims His newly clean people as best friends, who stirs them to want good things, and who helps them go after those good things, we will discover passions similar to His stirring in us.

None of us will sin in heaven, but not because it will be *impossible.* Sin will rather be *unthinkable.* Why? We will experience the passions of Christ fully and directly. Our Upper Room will be filled with such bright glory that the darkness of the Lower Room will vanish. The life of Christ will pour into us every moment from a fire hose. We will be in His literal, seeable presence.

No more thirst. No more self-doubt. No more unsatisfied longings. Only an Upper Room. We will then be a completely spiritual community, together journeying always deeper into the infinite heart of God, our chairs turned toward Him and each other at the same time.

For now, to catch a glimpse of Christ and to feel a trickle of His life pour into us, we must turn toward each other, toward spiritual friends and spiritual directors. As we turn, we can hope to give and receive small doses of the goodness of God.

Peter tells us that we are participants in the divine nature, and that we are thereby enabled to escape the corruption caused by Lower Room desires (see 2 Peter 1:3–4). When spiritual passions are aroused as our daughter walks in the door at three in the morning, we provide her with spiritual community. When spiritual passions are aroused when our counselee tells us he visited a topless bar three nights ago, we provide him with spiritual community.

And we will pour something powerful into each of these people through whatever words we say. It isn't something we manage. It's a reality we enjoy, as mystics.

I mentioned earlier that at a moment when Lower Room energy was all I could feel, I called a friend. I wanted an infusion of Christ. I wanted to experience His passions toward me. My friend celebrated me, believed in me, saw evidence of both the Spirit and the flesh, and gave me whatever the Spirit stirred him to give. My Upper Room passions were ignited. He stimulated me to love and good deeds.

Just yesterday, this same friend called me. "I don't think I'd be calling you now if you hadn't called me earlier."

He described a crisis point in his life that he regarded as monumental. That was the word he used. "I normally try to handle my most private, hardest battles on my own. But I really want to tell you what I'm dealing with. I'm not sure why."

I think he was hungry for spiritual passions to be aroused in me and poured into him. Because it happened the other way around, he knew it was possible.

He wanted soul food.

The conversation was not managed, although I was aware of my inclination to do so. What I gave him that was best I understand least. All I know is that New Covenant truth, pondered and enjoyed, roused divine passions in me that were felt in our conversation.

Of course, Lower Room passions were not, and are not destroyed. The snakes will bite again. Spiritual community, like breakfast, needs to be a daily affair. But both conversations were mystical moments when very ordinary language carried extraordinary passion into our souls.

Perhaps a model that loosely captures a strategy for becoming a mystical community, for developing the safest place on earth, will help. But first, we must make sure we are willing to move toward spiritual community. There is a price.

CHAPTER 15

It's Worth
the Risk

People who bore one another should meet seldom; people who
interest one another, often.—C. S. Lewis

Friends of mine finally persuaded their elderly mother to see a doctor. It had been well over a decade since her last visit. Previous efforts at persuasion were countered with, "Why should I see a doctor? I feel fine."

Finally, she relented, reluctantly, and with only a thin veneer of anger covering her fear.

Routine examination revealed trouble. More tests led to the diagnosis of cancer, and surgery and probable chemotherapy were prescribed. The angry veneer thickened.

"I should never have gone. I was getting along just fine without that doctor, and now I have to endure all those procedures."

Her logic is not unlike ours. If we keep distance from one another, if we never take a close look at what is going on in us and between us as we relate, we really do feel better. For a time. Sometimes for a long time.

When the possibilities inherent in spiritual community are even dimly apprehended, we are both terrified and galvanized. It's a place where something bad might be seen that, once surfaced, must be dealt with. But it's also a place where resurrection follows death, where real life is stirred up and can be enjoyed as never before, where the taste of life now whets our appetite for what lies ahead.

Spiritual community is at once the safest place on earth and the place of greatest danger.

A similar idea was apparently in Lewis's mind when he wrote *The Chronicles of Narnia*. Lucy, a visitor to the strange world of oppression and hope, was about to cross a bridge. But the great lion Aslan stood in her way. To reach her destination, she had to pass by the lion, within paw's length.

Lucy turned to a resident of the land who knew the lion well. "Is he safe?" she asked.

"Safe?" Mr. Tummis laughed. "No, he's not safe, but he's good."

When we enter spiritual community, we climb through the wardrobe into the Community of the Lion. Eventually we discover the Lion is a Lamb, but not until we've been shaken to our core by a few loud roars.

I just finished a phone conversation with a friend who told me that during a season of heavy trial in his life, he became a deist to preserve some kind of faith. He had prayed fervently, relentlessly, about a difficult matter, and things turned out badly, the exact opposite of his prayers. The Lion roared: "I will not help you as you want. Instead, you will feel my claws ripping your flesh."

It was easier for this man to believe in a watchmaker who started the clock ticking then backed away than in a sovereign, loving God who could make things better and did not.

When we make the choice to cross the bridge into spiritual community, for example, with our kids or best friend, we can count on trouble. Some things will go poorly. Becoming a Christian is one thing. Following Christ is another, especially when He tells us to get involved with other Christians. That's when the fuss begins.

Eventually, spiritual community confronts us with our most troublesome fear. It surfaces the gaping hole in our hearts and exposes all our futile attempts to fill it. It leaves us wondering if perhaps our worst terror is not a child's nightmare but a hideous reality. Maybe no one does love us. Maybe that hole will never be filled. Could it be that there is no love in this world? No place to belong where we fit and matter? No person who wants us? Talk to a recently divorced man. At one time or another, we all encounter pain like his. The difference is that he has a harder time disguising it.

Spiritual community can seem to tease us. The trickle of true life that enters our soul arouses hope. Then the stream dries up. Our best friend doesn't call. Our spouse speaks an unkind word. Our small group seems less interested in our ongoing and admittedly tiresome problems. We switch back and forth between hating them and hating ourselves. Maybe the problem is really in us. Maybe it is us. Perhaps we really are unlovable and unable to love.

When that thought occurs to us, we panic.

We were stupid to get our hopes up and allow someone to know us beneath the facade, even stupider to give what was most tender within us. We just got trampled on. It led nowhere good.

So many married couples have told me, "Every time we try to communicate, to really share who we are and be there for each other, things get worse. It's easier to watch more television." Suggestions about how to communicate better never seem to resolve the problem, not in their marriages or mine.

Do we really want to move into spiritual community? Do we want to stumble through the necessary confusion and to enter a place where every tension is more keenly felt?

Look around you. The happiest people seem to be the least involved in substantive, deeply personal community. Country clubs with golf tournaments, dinner dances, and membership campaigns are pleasant. Country club churches where the dues are voluntary and tax-deductible are even better. Congeniality has its appeal.

But those who catch a vision of what community could be have a hard time enjoying shallow community as they once did. I remember years ago having the chance to drive a Bentley around the block. It was tough returning to my Toyota Corolla.

People who want the most out of community typically feel the most disappointed. They are the ones who experience the full sting of betrayal, who notice the little snubs and can't get over them. Greater pain in relationship may evidence higher vision more than it does immaturity. "*I should never have gone to see that doctor.*"

I sometimes think that, if I could, I would be smart to only enjoy whatever is enjoyable about life, about me and other people. Perhaps if I numbed myself to the tensions and distance and awkwardness in my relationships, with a shoulder-shrugging "That's the way it is," I might be better off.

The old hymn, with a little editing, comes to mind:

> *Count your many blessings*
> *Name them one by one*
> *And pretend you're happy*
> *With what God has done.*

Unfortunately *I can't do it.* I can't deny what I want. I was built for more. My deepest desires are from God. And worse, I don't *want* to run from my heart. The yearnings of my inmost being sometimes feel like an enemy I've invited into my house.

And then I hear the gospel at a new level. I've been forgiven for my arrogance in trying to make it on my own, without community, without depending on God and without involving myself with people. I've been given a new identity as a unique contributor to the community of God. I can draw out of others what is uniquely best in them and they can do the same for me. I can't deny my longing to be seen and honored, celebrated, and enjoyed; and now I have something in me worth celebrating. And there's a power within me that keeps me headed in good directions.

Rachael and I had dinner last evening with Randy and Marcia. It was Marcia's birthday. My word-gift to her was *celebration.* The more my wife and I know her, the more we celebrate the miracle of her spiritual uniqueness. Randy agrees. We all felt joy.

It takes some reflection, but when I think about it, the dangers of community seem better to me than the dull safety of independence. Only what is bad is endangered in spiritual community. Even the failure of others can be turned to advantage. I can get a clearer look into myself as I observe my response and see what Lower Room passions need to be trotted out before the firing squad and what Upper Room passions call for a party.

In my pain, I will meet the snakes of pride and demandingness, but that meeting will increase my zeal to find the better place in me, and in my frustrating friends. When we connect with Upper Room passion, to ruin the meter of another old hymn, "it will be worth it all, when we see Jesus in each other."

Still, I'm scared. I hesitate. I write about spiritual community sitting in a hotel room by myself. I've been here several days. Carrie brings lunch to my room. We exchange pleasantries for less than a minute. She asks me how the book is coming. I tell her I appreciate her interest. I can handle that level of involvement. And it does feel good. Nothing deep is nourished, it's cotton candy fellowship, but it has its momentary sweetness.

It's when I think about going after more that the fear comes. Maybe there is no more, maybe cotton candy is all there is. I sometimes worry that my pursuit of truly spiritual community is like Dorothy's search for Oz. Will I find only a short, bald man hiding behind a screen creating an illusion of what never was?

My fear is strong enough to make me wonder if the epitaph on my grave will read: "Here lies a fool. He spent his life pursuing a fantasy." When I saw a stage performance of *Don Quixote* a year ago, the fear surfaced strongly. I could barely sit through the play till its finish.

Torturing questions battered my mind. Am I pompously riding a wooden horse through the Christian countryside slaying dragons that aren't there? Am I tilting at windmills, in a crusade that has no point? Should I stop wanting more? Should I simply go to church, meet nice people, sing good music, listen to decent preaching, cooperate with believers in causes I agree are important? Shall I let go of this mystical idea that we could actually "pour Christ" into one another and become inflamed with the Spirit's power?

I think I realize that there is no such thing as perfect community. Compared to Trinitarian standards, nothing any of us has seen comes close. We must be realistic. Howard Hendricks is on target when he says, "If you find a perfect church, don't join it. You'll ruin it."

I understand that, but . . .

We can do better. And we don't *have* to, we *want* to! God has given us everything we need to develop substantial spiritual community, if not with many, then at least with a few. Most of us are not coming close. The tragedy is that many Christians think they are.

It was the old people who had seen Solomon's temple who wept when the remnant from captivity laid the dismal foundations for a new one. The young folks were thrilled. They had no idea what a glorious temple looked like. They were satisfied with less (Ezra 3:10–13).

God told the old folks to face their discouragement: "Who of you is left who saw this house in its former glory? . . . Does it not seem to you like nothing? But now be strong . . . and work. For I am with you. . . . The glory of this present house will be greater than the glory of the former house" (Hag. 2:3–9 NIV).

The glory is now in us. The glory that first filled the tabernacle, then Solomon's temple, and then withdrew from the temple in the days of Ezekiel (see Ezek. 10) is now dwelling in the new temple, the body of Christ, in individual Christians who are to display that glory by the way they relate (1 Cor. 6:19).

If you have caught a glimpse of what community could be and find yourself weeping over what community now is, God's word to you is this: "Be strong. Don't give up. I am with you. The glory of the spiritual community is being slowly revealed and will one day fill the heavens. Never settle for less."

If your heart cries out for an experience of Christ that changes the way you relate to others, the Spirit is carrying your groans to the throne room. God's answer *may* require that we patiently seek out a few people who are weeping over the present state of Christian community and will risk everything to see the glory revealed. It *may* require that we disturb some parts of the evangelical establishment by not cooperating with their efforts to achieve less.

But it *will* certainly require that we remain involved with certain folks we'd prefer to avoid or permanently leave. Getting along with fellow

Starbucks lovers is easy. Offering spiritual community to hard-to-enjoy relatives and friends is not.

In any serious attempt to build true community, we will wrestle with confusion, disappointment and, occasionally, excruciating agony of soul. Those struggles will compel us to fix our eyes on unseen reality—the Spirit *is* at work, and to believe in a better day ahead—Christ *is* coming back.

Our journey together to God will bring us to a point where a choice among three options must be made.

1. *Go mad:* Keep trying to make present community completely satisfying.
2. *Back up:* The search for intimacy is too risky, too dangerous, with uncertain and meager rewards. Find a comfortably safe distance from people, wrap yourselves in a Christian blanket, and live there, safe and smug.
3. *Journey on:* Stay involved, not everywhere, with everyone, but somewhere, with a few. Don't give up on at least a couple of relationships. Die every day to your demand for total fulfillment now, in anything. Accept the ache in your soul as evidence of maturity, not neurosis. Discover the spiritual passions beneath the ache that are strong enough to sustain you in forward movement and to keep heaven in sight. If you put all your eggs in the basket of present community, even at its best, you will be of all men most miserable. Freely lust after the day that is coming. Let that hope keep you on course. Expect to discover the point of this life and to experience the spiritual joys available now, to get an unforgettable taste of Christ, to feel the Father's arms around you, to feel the Spirit within you.

If you choose the third option, then let me offer a simple model for engaging with people that may help us steer our way through stormy waters to a true experience of spiritual community.

If we turn our chairs, perhaps a few others will too.

CHAPTER 16

ENTER, SEE, TOUCH:
A Way of Developing Spiritual Community

*I had been received with open arms, given all the attention and affection
I could ever hope for, and offered a safe and loving place to grow
spiritually as well as emotionally. Everything seemed ideal. But precisely
at that time, I fell apart—as if I needed a safe place to hit bottom.*

—Henri Nouwen

Perhaps that's a good definition of *spiritual community*—"a safe place to hit bottom."

We all need a place safe enough to embrace our brokenness, our failure, and our inability to cope, and, in the midst of torment, a place to again discover life. I spend so much energy refusing to hit bottom. It terrifies me to think I'm in over my head, that I cannot pull it off.

I wonder how many of us never come to grips with how small and helpless we are. Brokenness is not attractive, not until we're broken in a safe place.

Until we experience the life of Christ poured into us, perhaps directly by our tender Father through His Spirit, often through His Word or a song, not frequently enough by our brothers and sisters, until then we don't understand joy.

To be broken in the midst of spiritual community brings a quality of rest and hope that cannot be duplicated. Feeling in control, of course, brings its own kind of peace. But it's never a *giving* peace. And it leaves a latent terror asleep, like a coiled snake ready to spring if disturbed.

Brokenness lets us feel that terror. When we admit, deeply and emotionally, that we cannot control what we most want, overwhelming horror sweeps into our soul. We feel nothing deeper. The dark night of the soul begins. We lower our head, retreat into the safety of aloneness, and wail in sheer agony. It's impossible to believe that sheer delight is waiting to greet us. Someone else needs to believe it for us.

If we get with a friend, if we embrace all that we are in another's presence, in the presence of someone who listens to the Spirit, soon we discover that *the lights went out only in the Lower Room.*

There is another room, a better one, and even as we continue to wail, we realize our Upper Room is softly illumined, only by a simple candle but with a flame that cannot be snuffed.

It may take days, months, even years to adjust our eyes to the gentle light. We're so used to the neon billboards of Las Vegas that candlelight in a quiet room seems dim, even unappealing. If we could return to the dazzling lights of a bright Lower Room, we would. In His mercy, the Spirit keeps that room dark, often by seeming not to hear us as we pray. He walls us in so we cannot get our life together as we want. He leads us into the desert.

Eventually we pray, tentatively at first, pleadingly, without much confidence. But then we notice that our prayers shift from prayers of *petition* to prayers of *communion.* Being with God becomes a pleasure, at some point our chief delight. Jealous feelings toward people more blessed seem to weaken as we learn to sit quietly in His presence, to *value* quietness with God.

The Bible suddenly means more. We read that nothing can separate us from Christ's love and we fall to our knees: "Lord, You're beautiful!" We've never said it before, not with quite that passion. Deep in our hearts, we begin to realize we're worshiping, we're delighting in God, we're in the Presence, and eavesdropping on the Trinity as They talk about us.

"I chose him."

"I died for him."

"I'm still working on him."

"He's Ours! It's almost time for the party!"

Trust seems natural; we find ourselves wanting to be like Christ. Hang the price—we'll pay anything! Obedience becomes a joy, a privilege. We want to do right. Will suffering help? Bring it on! The first chapter of James finally makes sense.

We lose interest in our own well-being; we feel like a beggar seated at a lavish buffet. "Eat all you want," our host commands.

"Can I go tell my friends? Freddie hasn't had a decent meal in months."

Concern for our wounds, for all the memories of abuse and neglect and public shame that we've worked so hard to soothe or forget, seem silly. Wounds? Yes, life has been terrible. But I'm whole. Why would I need to work through all of that?

We feel directed toward others with no thought of how they have treated us before or might again treat us. Self-protection, self-preservation, and self-enhancement are swept away by a quiet flood of love streaming out of our hearts. And that pouty demand that life should go as we think it should, along with the nagging sense that we're just not doing something quite right, is elbowed aside by the thrill of being alive.

We see Lower Room passions for what they are—cheap, dirty, stupid, worthy only of disdain. *They lose their hold on us.*

We look at others differently, both the people we like and those we don't. No longer are they objects to use with our needs in view, nor threats to guard against. We now see people as reasons for celebration, as possibilities in the making, as fellow strugglers who sometimes fail miserably and do the darndest things, as opportunities to give and receive our common life in Christ.

We experience a moment of spiritual community.

And then we wake up. Only a dream, a pleasant one, an ecstatically thrilling one, but . . . only a dream. Or was it? No, *it happened!* And if it hasn't happened to you yet, a cloud of witnesses will tell you it's real. I am among them.

Spiritual community is a reality. It can be our experience, perhaps for the first time, more often and intensely if we've already tasted it.

But it begins in brokenness. There is no other way. In God's economy, death always precedes resurrection. And the death of brokenness happens only in safe community. We hit bottom only when we find the safest place on earth.

So, what shall we do? How then shall we live? Let me now pull together everything I've so far said in this book and present my vision of the pathway to spiritual community, where ghosts become solid, where indestructible life is tasted, where safety is felt. Remember, though, at best we'll only get a taste. The banquet comes later.

First, a brief word to those in spiritual leadership. I agree with Eugene Peterson that the job of the pastor is to teach people to pray, to lead Christians into worship. Everything else—evangelism, discipleship, youth ministry, *everything*—flows from worship.

And I would affirm, strongly, that only a *worshiping* community will ever become a *connecting* community. We must meet God before we can share Him with others. A group of people who first connect with God and then pour into each other the passions that gush out of that encounter becomes a spiritual community.

Worship is of first-order importance. But that is not my topic. My burden is to think about the community that develops among worshipers.

What would it mean for a father to offer his unmarried pregnant daughter the gift of community? What would it mean for an offended friend to offer his offender the gift of community? What does spiritual community look like, and how could it develop, between husband and wife, parent and child, good friends, pastor and parishioner, counselor and counselee?

And how about groups larger than two? What is necessary for a family unit or a pastoral staff or an elder board or a worship team or a prayer coordination committee or a Bible study class or a small group or a team of workers in parachurch ministry to become a spiritual community?

What I have in mind can only happen among a handful of people, up to ten, maybe fifteen. The group must be small enough for each person's chair to turn toward the others. In a large group, that can't happen.

Other things, just as vital, can take place when more people assemble together. Thousands of saints can worship together, receive instruction, be challenged and inspired to deeper commitment, and join to make a dent in culture. But they can't become a community. In community, people know each other. They have turned their chairs to see one another, to listen, and occasionally to speak.

We are wrong to define only the Sunday morning event as *church*, and to treat small groups as an option, as an add-on that some might want to do in addition to "going to church." I prefer to think of the preaching/worship service as an important time in itself, as an opportunity to encounter God, but also as preparation for spiritual community, as a prelude to journeying more closely together in the right direction. Both define church.

The point of church is journeying together to God. So, what do we do?

Start with Prayer

Spiritual community is always a miracle. It cannot be programmed into existence. It will never be successfully scheduled to take place on Tuesday evening when the small group meets. Yet we still try to *manage* community. We end up settling for either an occasionally convincing counterfeit of community, where all that's missing is the Spirit, or we lose hope that we'll ever experience the real thing. And, of course, we won't—not as long as we stay in control. Lower Room passions never generate anything spiritual.

We must therefore pray. We're commanded to *wait on the Lord*. Because God's law is in us, we should hear that command the way a child hears his mother order him to eat a cookie, no, two cookies, no, all he wants.

But, the truth is, that's often *not* how we hear the command to wait on God in prayer. Many of us have been waiting for years to experience spiritual community, and we've just about given up. Church for many of us means choir practice, teaching sixth-grade girls, attending services and leaving feeling entertained, hyped up, scolded, heavy, or, for most, a little bored and disappointed.

Noah spent forty days cooped up in an enclosed boat with a few family members and enough animals to start a zoo, and he waited. (I wonder if he could keep track of time in the ark.) When finally it landed, Noah sent out a dove to see if it would find a dry place to rest. Or would it return, indicating it had found nothing but a world of water?

It returned. We're told that Noah ". . . reached out his hand and took the dove and brought it back to himself in the ark" (Gen. 8:9 NIV). I might have been tempted to wring its neck in frustration: *How much longer must I stay in here?*

But Noah *waited* (Hebrew *yachal*) seven more days. *Yachal* means "to wait expectantly, to wait with hope." Then he sent the dove out again. This time it flew back with a "freshly plucked olive leaf" in its mouth. The waters were receding, slowly. They had at least dipped below the level of tree branches, but it was not yet time to open the hatch.

Noah waited another full week. He was waiting to walk out of the boat onto dry land, not mud.

Prayer is *expectant* waiting. But we're not good waiters. We're more like King Ahab who, after three years of famine, decided he was through waiting. "Why should I wait [*yachal*] for the LORD any longer?" (2 Kings 6:33 NIV). How often we cry, "How long, O Lord, how long?" but with a spirit that says, "I've waited long enough. God's not going to do anything."

Sometimes the Lion roars, "Wait longer."

Sometimes the Lamb whispers, "Your waiting is over. Enjoy My blessing!"

Many of us have been waiting for years to experience true community. We long to know and be known, to feel the joys of freedom and love and intimacy. Many of us are worn out from calling for help. The waters of circumstantial suffering and deep torment have risen neck-high and our eyes see no evidence of God. We're tired of wet pillows every morning.

The psalmist knew that experience. But he waited for God: "But I pray to you, O LORD" (Ps. 69 NIV; see especially v. 13). And he rested in the prospect of God's *sure* salvation.

Habakkuk found the strength to "wait patiently" for God to reveal His power on behalf of Israel, even to the point of rejoicing in the Lord when everything around him fell apart (Hab. 3:16–18).

We so easily pray for what we know we cannot control: "God, heal my wife of cancer." And we work on what we still think we can control: "OK, here's our plan to develop small groups. Does everyone have a manual? Good. Oh, yes, let's open in prayer."

Nouwen once pointed out that our approach to prayer is so different from our Lord's. When He lived here, He prayed *first*, sometimes all night. Then He gathered a community around Himself. *Then* He sent them out to minister. We have it backward. We plan what we want to happen, complete with vision statements, short-term and long-term goals, and strategic initiatives, *then* we organize a team to help make it happen. And finally, with our plans in place, we commit them to the Lord.

Spiritual community starts with prayer.

Lay the Foundation

Remember the three foundational convictions I discussed in chapter 12.

1. *Growth is a mystery.*

   Give up managing growth and assume the head-down posture of humility. Give up any claim to power over another person's life. That means your child, your spouse, and your friend who is doing foolish things. We can't help anyone, including ourselves. We never manage the spiritual life. We rather flow with it. Spiritual community develops only among humble people.

2. *Personal holiness counts for more than trained skill.*

   Get whatever training you can in counseling or spiritual direction or parenting or small group leadership, but realize that training without character does no good. Realize, too, that character without training does great good, and, that character plus training might add a little. Spiritual community develops only among people who seriously value personal holiness.

3. *Every felt desire is, at root, a longing for God, though often unrec-ognized as such.*

The sexual addict walking into the adult bookstore is looking for God. The corporate climber salivating over another big close wants God. Most of us have never gotten a good taste of God, so we get excited about less.

And it's important to realize that we never create a desire for God in anyone; we rather see that it's already there in His children and stir it up. We honor the reality of desire. It's the pathway to God. Spiritual community develops only among people who aren't afraid to want, who honor desire, who feel it in themselves and learn to arouse it in others.

Grasp God's Truth

The centerpiece of biblical revelation is Jesus Christ. From Genesis to Revelation, it's all about Him. He made known the Father, He brought grace and truth after Moses brought the Law, and He sent the Spirit to reveal more of who He is to us. It was He who introduced, established, and now, by His Spirit, services the contract God made with us. That contract is called the New Covenant.

Spiritual community exists only when *spiritual* passions stir in our being more deeply than *fleshly* passions. But those passions—worship, trust, growth, obedience—have no existence apart from the New Covenant. A. W. Tozer makes the point that "the only healthy emotions are those aroused by great ideas."[1]

At least four great ideas make up the New Covenant. They are the four provisions we've already noted.

1. Our *new purity* that arouses *worship* toward God and *celebration* toward others.
2. Our *new identity* that arouses *trust* in God and the *envisioning* of others.
3. Our *new disposition* that arouses an eagerness to *grow* in Christ and a wise *discernment* of one another's hearts.

4. Our *new power* that arouses the passion to *obey* and joy in *giving* to others what the Spirit makes alive in us when we're with them.

Let me put it all together in a diagram:

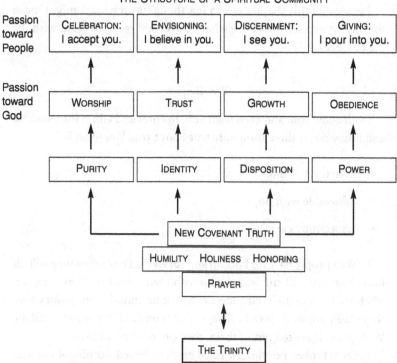

THE STRUCTURE OF A SPIRITUAL COMMUNITY

Passion toward People	CELEBRATION: I accept you.	ENVISIONING: I believe in you.	DISCERNMENT: I see you.	GIVING: I pour into you.

Passion toward God	WORSHIP	TRUST	GROWTH	OBEDIENCE

PURITY	IDENTITY	DISPOSITION	POWER

NEW COVENANT TRUTH

HUMILITY   HOLINESS   HONORING

PRAYER

THE TRINITY

That, as I see it, is the dynamic *structure* of spiritual community. Let me now suggest the *process* it creates, what we actually do to create the safest place on earth. The process has three parts:

1. We *enter* each other's lives with celebration and with the message: *I accept you!*

2. We *see* what's beneath the surface, what could be and what is, both good and bad. We communicate the message: I believe in you and I discern both the Spirit's work and the work of the flesh in your life.

3. We *touch* each other with the life of Christ; we freely give whatever the Spirit incites within us as we get to know each other. Our message is: I give you whatever the Spirit stirs me to give you.

Let me end this chapter with a few thoughts on what it might mean to *enter* someone's life, to *see* what's there, and to *touch* them with the life of Christ.

We Enter

I will allow you, and even want you, to enter and climb into my soul and know me, if three things are true about you. You must be:

- Broken yet strong

- Vulnerable with hope

- Respectfully curious

Broken people have hit bottom and survived. They know they will hit lower bottoms still and will rise up with even more life. They are overwhelmed by both their selfishness and their neediness to the point where they gladly admit their radical dependency on God. No one else will do. With pride squeezed out of them, they can only plead mercy.

Because broken people have faced death and lived, nothing about who they are is at stake when they engage with others. They don't *have* to be helpful or clever or appreciated. When they interact with us, we realize they are not working to make anything happen.

Brokenness has humbled them. We feel no pressure to cooperate with some effort to change us. They *want* us to change, to grow, to mature, but we don't have to change for their sakes. Whether we change or not, they remain solid. We can hurt them but we cannot destroy them. We don't make them nervous. Therefore, we feel safe.

The broken people I know seem more aware of their inadequacies than their strengths, but not with a "poor me, take-care-of-me" attitude. *They* feel their neediness. *We* feel their strength.

Broken people always find reason to worship God and to celebrate us. We don't feel used by them because their center is already solid. With their new purity clearly in view, they never ask us to finally validate them. That's already been done.

Broken people can say hard things and we appreciate it, because they find no joy in the power of superior knowledge or superior morality. They take no pleasure in their being right and our being wrong. God's glory matters to them, and it matters more than anything else. They are not proud of their wisdom. They don't put their insight on display to win applause.

And they are vulnerable, not indiscriminately but meaningfully. Their self-disclosure doesn't feel self-preoccupied. When they share their struggles, we know we're invited in but not to help, not to feel sorry for all they endure, but rather to hope together.

Out of their brokenness and vulnerability, the people we want to be entered by are insatiably but respectfully curious, never invasive, but eagerly willing to walk through whatever doors we open. Their next sentence doesn't *miss* what we've just said nor is it *controlled* by our last remark. Sometimes, while they listen to us, they look away, or perhaps close their eyes. Their focus is on Someone else. We're not their final interest. Without feeling pushed or pressured, we feel drawn into another plane, toward another Person, as they continue to ask us questions.

We feel safe with folks who are: (1) broken yet strong, (2) vulnerable with hope, and (3) respectfully curious. They worship God and, because of what they know about Him, they celebrate us. We feel more solid in their presence.

We See

Spiritual communities see our new identities and what we could therefore become. They also see what the Spirit is up to at this moment in our lives, prodding our new inclinations, and how Lower Room passions are working to thwart the process. Seeing, then, has two parts: *envisioning* and *discerning*.

Envisioning

Humble, holy, broken people love themselves, but they pay scant attention to it. They know they have eternal value and they respect the unique contributions they make to God's purposes.

My recent time in Quebec City was a new experience for me of feeling important and humble at the same time. A woman I know slid into the chair next to me after I preached in her church. We've chatted and corresponded off and on for perhaps ten years.

"I want you to know," she said, "you do something for me that no one else does. Others do what you cannot do, but you have a unique place in my life." I was thrilled, mostly by the fact that I felt more grateful than puffed up. My focus stayed more on her joy than mine.

Lewis made a similar point:.

> In each of my friends there is something that only some other friend can fully bring out. By myself, I am not large enough to call the whole man into activity; I want other lights than my own to show all his facets. In this, Friendship exhibits a glorious nearness to Heaven itself where the very multitude of the blessed (which no man can number) increases the fruition which each has of God. For every soul, seeing Him in her own way, doubtless communicates that unique vision to all the rest.[2]

Spiritual friends see a facet of Christ in us and bring it out as no one else can. And they delight to do so. When they see what is unique about us, it causes them great delight; and then, giving way to the powers of daring imagination, they envision what we could become. The vision excites them—with Paul, they see us where we are and feel pains of labor till Christ is formed in us (Gal. 4:19).

Discerning

Seeing involves more than envisioning someone in their new identity and what they could become. It also includes a sensitivity to the

Spirit's present, immediate activity in that person's life, surfacing and stirring up new appetites.

In spiritual community, not only are people celebrated and envisioned, they're also recognized; good things and bad things are discerned and brought to light. Friends, and especially spiritual directors, pay close attention to the impact others have on them.

Something about us thrills them, when, for example, they see us becoming kinder, and they delight to say so, knowing they've caught a glimpse of the Spirit at work. When something troubles them, they take it seriously, as a doctor would when discerning a dark spot on an x-ray. Without compulsion, without pushing, without condescending, and without requiring agreement or action from us, they sometimes point it out and wait to see if we open the door to further exploration.

Perhaps at that moment, when our spiritual community disrupts us with an exposure of where we're blindly wrong, we most sense their trust in God to grow us. They are humble, broken people who know growth is God's mysterious work and that their commitment to personal holiness is more powerful than strong rebuke. They may at times be firm. Discipline has its place. But they never push.

We Touch

Now we've felt the *safety of celebration,* the *hope of vision,* and the *wisdom of loving discernment.* We've been opened up to the work of God. We're ready to receive the *power of Christ's touch.*

Even though we've heard the Lion roar, we know the Lamb is leading gently. In personal conversation, a wise older friend once said to me, "Remember, Larry, Christ always leads gently." I had been hearing only the roar. His words brought rest.

Spiritual friends listen to God, they listen to what He is stirring in their own hearts as they engage with us. With a freedom only broken people know, they simply give that to us, whatever it is, as faithful messengers of God and lovers of our soul.

It may be a rebuke, a piece of homey advice, even a joke that occurs to them. It may be a thought from Scripture or a memory from their past they want to share. It's rarely clever, it rarely generates admiration of the messenger's brilliance, though it may create a longing to be similarly sensitive to God's Spirit. Whatever it is, whether a hard word or a warm hug, it comes from heaven to us through a member of Christ's body. And we *know* it.

Perhaps the most serious obstacle to touching each other is our reluctance to share what is most deeply alive in us, what we see as terrific. It's far easier to share interesting news about mutual friends and to gripe to a hopefully sympathetic audience than it is to express what is mystically most real in our hearts.

Perhaps we're afraid to expose something so precious for fear others will treat it as common. "So you had a great time with the Lord last night, a real moment of worship. That's great! I'll bet it had nothing to do with last Sunday's sermon. Wasn't the preacher awful?" We've paraded our baby to someone who didn't ooh and aah nearly enough; we've learned to be cautiously bashful with what thrills us most.

Spiritual people touch others because they are free. Their passion to obey God releases a willingness to give whatever is in them to give. They live with remarkable confidence that what is deepest within them comes from the Spirit. It is Christ. And they delight to make Him known.

As you prepare to meet with your small group next week, schedule an hour alone the night before. Visualize each person.

1. Ponder what it would mean for you to present yourself to them as a broken yet strong, vulnerable but hopeful, and respectfully curious person. With the passion to celebrate each one of them aroused within you, pray that you will be a safe person, someone they would want to enter them.

2. Then, as an act of trust, reflect on your unique value to a few people. You bring out goodness in a handful of others that no one else brings out. Notice how that makes you feel.

   Think of your group members. Imagine their uniqueness. Ask what they bring out in you that stays locked up with others. Put words to that uniqueness, then envision what each one could mean to the body of Christ as the Spirit more completely forms Christ in them.

3. Attend to your longing to grow. Where is the Spirit working in your life? What's getting in the way? Begin to reflect on how your friends are growing. What do you see that delights you? What makes you angry, disappointed, or sad? Pray for each one.

4. Still on your knees, pay close attention to whatever feels holy and living and passionate within you. Perhaps you want to write a letter to someone in the group. Maybe a song from the CD you just purchased comes to mind and you want to give someone your copy. Be obedient. Pour into each one what is alive in you.

Spiritual community develops as the passions of God's Spirit, aroused by the truth of the gospel, begin to flow between people as they relate. Don't stop getting together, and when you are together, think hard about how to stimulate one another to love and good deeds.

IT'S TIME TO TURN OUR CHAIRS TOWARD ONE ANOTHER

CHAPTER 17

Becoming
Spiritual Community

He works on us in all sorts of ways. But above all, He works on us
through each other. Men are mirrors, or "carriers" of Christ to other
men. Usually it is those who know Him that bring Him to others. That is
why the Church, the whole body of Christians showing Him to one
another, is so important. It is so easy to think that the Church has a lot
of different objects—education, building, missions, holding services. . . .
The Church exists for no other purpose but to draw men into Christ, to
make them little Christs. If they are not doing that, all the cathedrals,
clergy, missions, sermons, even the Bible itself, are simply a waste of
time. God became man for no other purpose. It is even doubtful, you
know, whether the whole universe was created for any other purpose.

—C. S. Lewis

As I prayed this morning for a friend going through rough times, an
image formed in my mind. I saw a Gibraltar-size rock emerging out
of a wild ocean. As the rock took its place, steady, solid, and thoroughly
settled, I could see frightened people floundering in the water looking
to the rock and finding hope.

The rock had a face. It was my friend. I began to cry; tears flowed out of deep parts within me as I realized the power of one man's life to bring drowning people to safety.

Then I thought about a group of people, each one a rock, enough to form an island, and my mind drifted to the beatitudes of Jesus. When He pronounced broken people blessed, the word He used that we translate "blessed" means an island, a quiet, undisturbed place of safety.

The community of God's people is to be that rock in stormy seas, an island of peace in a world of pain. It is to be the community of the broken: humble people who commune with God and depend on Him for everything good; repentant people who love holiness more than sin; passionate people who honor and search for and embrace their deepest desires because they know their desire is for God.

These rock-solid people have heard Jesus speak to the offended Pharisees when sinners gathered around Him: "It is not the healthy who need a doctor, but the sick" (Matt. 9:12 NIV). People who make up a spiritual community have taken their place as sick people, found the cure, and now long to spread the news that broken people can live.

One small church I know has welcomed a brain-damaged woman into their fellowship, a rather straightforward but tender woman who sometimes speaks up during the sermon to express her opinion. An elder told me they receive her as an angel, as a person sent from God to call out of them deeper levels of compassion and grace than they otherwise might have known was in them.

Another church has a young woman who recently confessed her sin to the fellowship. The consequences and pain continue, but the love and hope are real. Her father knelt before his daughter in tears, crying out in his anguish as he gave himself to her.

In the middle of the wild ocean of shattered dreams and broken lives, the community of Christ celebrates God's forgiveness; they believe in what each other could become, they never minimize sin but they love to maximize grace. They are carriers of Christ to each other. That's what spiritual friends do when they act together to journey to God.

But sometimes we need more. Our lives can become messy, a fog can roll in so thick that we can't see even one step ahead. Special guidance may be called for. There are times when it's good to ask a wise person to turn his or her chair toward us, to look deeply into our hearts, to help us gain perspective, to see what we're too blind to see, and to uncover what in our self-deceiving ways we hide from ourselves.

Sometimes a spiritual friend isn't enough—we need a *spiritual director.*

How do we handle the choke hold Lower Room passions sometimes have on us? What do we do with deep depression, compulsive addictions, and uncontrollable panic? What *should* we do with our neglecting or abusive spouse, our introverted child who has no friends, our friend who struggles with homosexual urges? How do we respond to disappointments that crush our souls and leave us angry, near despair, and ready to quit?

Spiritual friends may enter our lives with celebrating love, move into us with the hope of vision, see patterns we should continue and some that should end, and give us powerful input that reflects Christ. But more discernment may be needed than good friends have. It might be time to lay our lives before a wise man or woman who is specially called to the ministry of spiritual direction.

Most people agree on the need for wise people to talk with, but our culture has a strange way of providing them. The process is self-selecting and the preparation is academic. Those who sense a burden to help people think right away of the counseling profession. They apply to graduate schools, they send in recommendations from former professors and a few friends with noteworthy credentials certifying their aptitude for such work. They take tests to demonstrate adequate gray matter and then spend several years in classrooms, studying counseling theory and technique.

Where is the church in the process?

When these individuals finish their degree, a state board, upon successful completion of an exam, tells society that they have enough knowledge—even though they are often quite young—to competently practice psychology, and I suppose they do. But when I struggle with life, I don't want a technician applying psychological principles to my life. I want a wise, seasoned, spiritual saint who can peer into my soul and direct me, through all that's there, toward God.

Competence to care for souls and to cure them, to nurture the work of the Spirit in another's life, depends first on spiritual maturity, on the depth of the helper's communion with God. Folks who sense a call to this work need more than merely to be accepted into graduate studies by an admissions committee. They should be affirmed by a godly community who agree that indeed this person has been called.

Competence to provide care and cure for souls depends on a rich and growing familiarity with all that God has revealed, about life and people and what's wrong with us and what He is doing about it. A spiritual community, not merely an academic one, is the proper breeding ground for spiritual directors.

Western culture has wrongly divided the territory into spiritual problems and psychological problems. We assign pastors and nice Christian people to deal with the first sort. They pray, discuss biblical passages, apply biblical principles, and nourish faith. Trained specialists are called in if the problem is thought to be psychological, something emotionally or relationally disturbed that prayer and biblical exhortation don't seem to touch. We think of these disturbances as diseases and disorders of the psyche that therapists must treat.

But that's wrong. Psychological problems at root are spiritual problems. People suffering with them need spiritual counseling. (Certain symptoms may reveal a physical disorder, in which case neither therapist nor pastor can help. A physician is needed.) But spiritual counseling is too often thought of as superficial, structured discipleship: Memorize these verses, pray more, stop doing that, and don't miss church.

In my view, spiritual counseling (or spiritual direction) does everything we now assume can only be done in psychotherapy. It probes the darkness of our deceived and defensive hearts (the Lower Room). It looks for life that has survived terrible assaults (the Upper Room). It enters the depths of pain and agony (the groaning of Rom. 8). And it provides an opportunity to relate in ways that heal (the stimulating toward love and good deeds of Heb. 10:24).

The choice is not between psychotherapy and spiritual direction. It is rather between independence and community. It is a choice between going it alone out of fear and pride *or* journeying toward God in a group, with love from spiritual friends and special wisdom from spiritual directors.

I have taught graduate counseling for nearly twenty years. My earnest conviction is that we would do well to discard the vocabulary of professionalism, to no longer speak of patients, diagnosis, treatment, and psychotherapy. The very same concerns would be better and more powerfully addressed if instead we talked about souls disconnected from God, themselves, and others; about soul care and soul cure; about spiritual discernment into the workings of Flesh Dynamics and Spirit Dynamics; about spiritual friendship and spiritual direction.

The phrase "spiritual direction" carries some baggage. I don't use the term to imply that a *director* has the authority to tell someone else what to do. I refer, rather, to a mature saint called to serve others by pointing the way to God. Those who instruct others about whom to marry, what passage to read, and how many days to fast are on dangerous ground. They resemble leaders who lord power over their charges, people our Lord did not commend.

But no other term seems to carry less baggage. *Spiritual guide* has New Age connotations that blur the distinction between biblically informed guidance and whimsical ideas about what the Spirit might be saying, unrelated to what He has already said clearly in Scripture.

Therapist, an excellent word in its historical meaning of minister, smacks too much of the idea of gaining expertise through training. It doesn't convey the importance of spiritual depth as a primary qualification.

Counselor feels too anemic. A good word, but overused. Everybody counsels.

Mentor and *disciple* both have mechanistic overtones that miss the fluid dynamic of the Spirit's sovereign movement.

Elder too often means a person with business savvy and organizational ability.

Pastor conveys an image of someone you see and hear from once a week, and a little more often if you're in the hospital.

Teacher conjures images of classrooms, overhead projectors, and lecture outlines.

Shepherd comes closer and perhaps would do.

But, with reservation, I vote for the term *spiritual director.*

We are on a journey. Life is a journey toward a land we have not yet seen along a path we sometimes cannot find. It is a journey of the soul toward its destiny and its home. Spiritual directors are men and women who know the Spirit, who trust the Spirit, who by virtue of calling and gifting and self-awareness can see into the workings of the human soul and can direct it toward its end.

They read widely. Perhaps they have degrees in counseling; perhaps—and this might be better—in literature or philosophy. Perhaps they have little formal education. They love the Scriptures, revering them as God's Word, but they also read novels by Annie Dillard, Fyodor Dostoevsky, and John Grisham.

Above all, they do not manage their lives or the lives of others. They live as mystics, sensitive to the reality of Christ in them, anchored in the reality that they are in Christ. They are people who pray.

The training they most value has come from godly men and women, perhaps professors, perhaps pastors, perhaps plumbers or seamstresses, people who spoke to them about prayer and the Trinity and worship and grace. The informality of their most valuable training has taught them never to follow formulas, never to "do" counseling. They instinctively and intuitively engage with people as the Spirit directs them.

Not many of us have access to such a person. But time with a spiritual director could help scores of people—people like Maria.

Maria is a hemophiliac. She is single, in her early fifties, and desperately lonely. She struggles with undiagnosed chronic fatigue and feels uncomfortable with most people. Occasionally she senses a freedom with certain folks, but generally she prefers to be by herself.

To Maria, church feels routine and flat, more like a scolding than a cup of cold water. In her Sunday school class, the teacher opens with prayer requests that are rarely personal, never risky, and the teaching is formulaic: You do this and God will do that. She knows it doesn't work.

On and off, Maria struggles with depression, sometimes severe enough that she takes medication. At times she feels wildly tempted to fly to a big city and have sex with twenty men. More than once, she has had to fight off thoughts of suicide.

If Maria were in a spiritual community, her life could be different. If she found a place safe enough for her to hit bottom and still be celebrated, believed in, seen, and touched, she would experience a different reality within herself. Her Upper Room passions would be stirred.

But Maria, like most of us at difficult times in our lives, might need more. It would be good if a spiritual director were available to meet with her, maybe every day during a week of spiritual retreat, perhaps for an intensive few hours every few months, or maybe even on a weekly basis if the other two options were not possible.

But she has no one. Maria has no true spiritual community. Instead, she has only a few friends who offer her moments of congeniality over dinner, who invite her to cooperate with them on church projects, who sometimes try to console her with sincere empathy and then recommend she get counseling or, in their impatience, tell her to conform to biblical standards. There is no older woman or man she trusts to provide her with wisdom, at least none that are available to her.

It could be so different.

The church needs many things. But it will properly *prioritize* its needs only when it gets its *purpose* straight. Its purpose is to draw people into Christ, to mirror Christ to one another, to show Christ to others by the way we live.

That happens only in a community of people on a journey to God, only in a group of people who turn their chairs toward each other. Spiritual friends and spiritual directors are people filled with Christ's energy who have turned their chairs, who pour their passions into each other and invite others to join them on the porch. But not many people, particularly not many men, have one truly spiritual friend. Even fewer have access to a spiritual director.

If the Spirit is stirring you with thoughts of community, and you're wondering what we can do to develop spiritual communities filled with spiritual friends and sprinkled with spiritual directors, I invite you to join me in prayer to hear the mind of God, to see what He would have us do. I pray this book provides some help.

The church is meant to be a community of spiritual friends and spiritual directors who journey together to God. We must become that community. Prayer is the starting point.

Questions for Thought
and Discussion

Introduction:
Let's Turn Our Chairs

- Perhaps the Holy Spirit sees members of the church the way Dr. Crabb saw those people in Miami, lined up and sitting in rocking chairs, facing straight ahead with no life passing back and forth between them. When, if ever, have you done the fellowship things church folks do—"tell personal stories, share prayer requests, discuss interesting things, reflect on biblical texts, worship together, sometimes even weep for one another"—and yet felt that no real connection was happening? What do you think was missing—and why?

- Dr. Crabb holds out the vision of Christians experiencing "a kind of oneness that makes us aware of what's best inside us and of all the bad stuff that blocks its release, a *penetrating* oneness that releases nice little boys to be men and sweet little girls to be women." What is appealing to you about this vision? What is threatening? What could you do about your hesitation or fear?

- In Part I, Dr. Crabb will describe a way of thinking about spiritual community. At this point, before you read any further, what comes to mind when you hear the phrase "spiritual community"? What examples of spiritual community (as you think of it) have you heard of, seen, or perhaps even been a part of?

- In Part II, Dr. Crabb will develop a way of understanding our struggles that makes it clear why spiritual friends and spiritual directors are important to life's journey. Whom do you consider a spiritual friend? If you've ever had a spiritual director, how did you benefit? If you haven't, how might you benefit?

• Why did you pick up this book—because of an experience in the past, hunger in the present, or hope about the future? What, if anything, did the introduction make you long for?

Let's start laying the foundation for the nuts and bolts of Dr. Crabb's message—a way of relating in this world that defines what it means to be in spiritual community. Let's get ready to turn our chairs.

PART I

A Way of Thinking about Spiritual Community

CHAPTER 1

For God's Sake,
Don't Expect It to Be Easy

- Neither the goal of spiritual life nor the process involved is clearly understood: Exactly what does it mean to be whole and mature in Christ—and how do we get there? Apart from Jesus in the Bible, what model(s) of Christian maturity have you seen? Be specific about the evidence of spiritual maturity in that person's life.

- Confusion and disappointment are inevitable on the journey toward spiritual maturity. But the up side of confusion is openness, and the up side of disappointment is that it inspires hope by making it necessary. What confusion about living spiritually in an unspiritual world—about Christian maturity and how to attain it—have you experienced? What disappointments have you encountered along the way, disappointments that God is undoubtedly using to grow your faith and make you mature in Christ?

- Review Dr. Crabb's discussion of the "hot topics" surrounding his ideas (pages 6–10). What surprised you or taught you something new? With what points do you especially disagree and/or agree? Give one or two examples.

- Where are you in need of soul care? Why would Dr. Crabb suggest spiritual friendship and spiritual direction, instead of psychological counseling, for someone in need of soul care?

The only unconfusing and thoroughly nondisappointing fact in life is that Christ's atonement guarantees the Spirit's unstopping work in our lives, from conception through death and on into eternity. In that we find hope for a soul in need of care.

CHAPTER 2
It's Not Easy,
but It's Worth It

- Our natural foundations must be destroyed if true spirituality is to develop. And this happens when, in His bewildering mercy, God sometimes shatters our fondest dreams, or at least allows them to be shattered. In His sovereignly run universe, the unthinkable happens, the nightmare we thought we'd never have to face. When have your dreams been shattered? What nightmare have you had to face? What has prompted you to ask, "Who is this God I claim to love? And where is He?" What, if anything, can you see at this point of your life about how God is using these experiences to grow you toward spiritual maturity?

- Henri Nouwen wrote about his inner wound "that is so easily touched and starts bleeding again," saying, "It is there to stay, but maybe for a good reason. Perhaps it is a gateway to my salvation, a door to glory, and a passage to freedom." Share your thoughts about how a wound can be such a gift. Consider what kind of salvation, glory, and freedom a wound can lead to.

- The path to the joy of God's presence always leads through joyless isolation, when the part of us that most longs for connection is alone. When that happens, the nature of our spiritual community is revealed. When have you taken the kind of risk Dr. Crabb took and shared something of your self, your spiritual journey, and perhaps even your woundedness with someone or with a group of people? What reactions did you not want . . . what reaction did you hope for . . . and what reaction did you receive? What did you realize from that experience about the kind or degree of Christian community available to you?

- Dr. Crabb has given up on healing—on a repair job on what is wrong that will lessen his struggles. Instead he wants to focus more on finding God and less on solving problems, more on worshiping God in any circumstance and less on using God to improve his circumstances, more on a journey and less on pathology. Why do we so often experience the opposite and our focus switches from progressing spiritually to healing emotionally or improving things circumstantially? And when have you heard—or perhaps said—the kinds of sentences listed on pages 17–18, sentences that take us on a detour from knowing God and off the narrow road of glorifying Him?

- We're a community of fixers. We can't stand to see a problem we can't do something about. And we like to label each other's problems because labels give us a sense of control. We're not curious about how God might be at work, and we don't realize that life's valleys do not primarily represent problems to be solved, but rather are opportunities for spiritual companionship. What current circumstances in your life make you wonder how God is at work? What present situation is an opportunity for spiritual companionship?

- What did you find most stirring about Dr. Crabb's call in this chapter to build the church into a community of people who take refuge in God and encourage each other never to flee to another source of help?

A central task of community is to become a place safe enough for each of us to own our brokenness. Only then can the power of connecting do its job. Only then can community be used of God to restore our souls.

CHAPTER 3
Spiritual Community:
What It Is

- When have you been with a small group of believers and found your appetite for holy things stirred and your longing to know God become intense? What do you think contributed to that stirring? What, if anything, did you do about satisfying that appetite and fulfilling that longing?

- Henri Nouwen wrote, "I ponder my experience and I recognize once more that the way for us to be in this world is to focus on the spiritual life." When have you seen this focus on the spiritual life enable someone "to be in this world"? Ideally, give an example from your life, but an example from the life of someone you know may also be helpful.

- C. S. Lewis observed, "Put first things first and second things are thrown in. Put second things first and you lose both first and second things." Using this statement as a lens through which to look at your life, what does it suggest about your approach to current pain or problems? What might putting first things first (glorifying God through worship and trust being the first thing) look like in your present circumstances?

- Review Dr. Crabb's dialogue with his friend (pages 25–27), noting especially the analysis he provided afterward. What did you appreciate about Dr. Crabb's approach? What was new about this approach? Why could it be helpful?

• Dr. Crabb comments, "Counselors spend wasted time trying to improve what God has abandoned." In what situations might that be true? When God has abandoned an aspect in our life, what role can the Holy Spirit play in that room in our souls?

In a spiritual community, people reach deep places in each other's hearts that are not often or easily reached. They discover places beneath the awkwardness of wanting to embrace and cry and share opinions. They openly express love and reveal fear, even though they feel so unaccustomed to that level of intimacy. Spiritual togetherness creates movement. Togetherness in Christ encourages movement toward Christ.

CHAPTER 4
It Takes
an Armando

- We human beings too easily commit to safety *from* people and don't take the risks that might allow us to enjoy safety *with* people. Who in your life fits each category? More specifically, with whom do you feel the need to protect yourself and keep yourself safe? And with whom do you feel safe to share yourself, warts and all? Which list is longer? Why?

- It is our weakness, not our competence, that moves others; our suffering, not our blessings, that breaks down the barriers of fear and shame that keep us apart; our admitted failures, not our paraded successes, that bind us together in hope. When have you experienced this truth in your relationships? Be specific and consider why the connections happened perhaps rather unexpectedly.

- We often hear that brokenness is the pathway to a deeper relationship with God, but we rarely see it modeled. (Too often we want others to believe that we know God by demonstrating how together we are!) When have you seen brokenness lead to a deeper relationship with God? Offer an example from your own life, from the life of someone you know, or from the life of someone in the Bible.

- If we face ourselves fully, we will be broken by what we see, by the selfishness and fear and rage and lust that cover our spiritual beauty like tarnish on silver. But the silver is there. Labeling each other makes the shine of that silver hard to see. Labels also encourage us to believe that our problems define us. What labels have been given to you by others? What labels have you given to yourself? In what ways are these limits confining, limiting, or protecting you?

- Look back over the following passages. What lesson did these offer you personally?

  — The description of Armando and the bishop

  — Dr. Crabb's conversation with Rich

  — Dr. Crabb's response to Beth

A spiritual community consists of people who have the integrity to come clean. That happens only when we have the confidence that ugliness and conflict will not end a relationship, a confidence that grows out of an even stronger confidence that what is deepest within is not brokenness but beauty, the literal beauty of Christ.

CHAPTER 5
Unspiritual Community

- In unspiritual community, we tend either to hide our problems or to parade them (see the chapter's first three paragraphs). Which of these directions do you lean toward now or have you chosen in the past? Explain your choice and briefly describe how the community in which you did the choosing may have encouraged your choice.

- Maggie Ross describes the spiritual life as continually beginning to understand that loneliness is really a hunger for God. When in your life, if ever, have you sensed that truth for yourself? Or now, looking back on a lonely time, can you see that loneliness as a hunger for God? What did you do about your loneliness—or what are you doing about it now? What antidote to loneliness does defining it as "a hunger for God" suggest?

- Maggie Ross seems to go on to say that true relationship with each other (what Dr. Crabb calls connecting or spiritual community) is not possible without rich and abiding communion with God. What are you doing—or what could you be doing—to have "rich and abiding communion with God"? What do you find yourself *wanting* to do? Be specific.

- Human relationships inevitably encounter conflict, and only the resources of the Spirit are adequate to move us through conflict into true relationship. When have you let conflict serve as an opportunity to draw more fully on spiritual resources? Be specific about those resources and how they helped in the conflict. When has conflict been an opportunity for spiritual friendship to flourish? Give details about the friend and the kind of soul care he/she offered you. And when could a conflict you encountered have been an opportunity for you to connect with a spiritual director and experience soul care? How might the resolution of the conflict been different?

- Conflict is latent in every human relationship at every moment. It simply awaits a trigger, and our sin, self-occupied passions, and brokenness (broad categories all) serve as triggers. When, if ever, have you had this ugly, selfish side of you seen and accepted but not condoned by a friend, by a person who knows brokenness, who cares about you living well, who pours the life he or she has received from God into you? Or when have you been able to extend such gracious acceptance to another? In what ways does such acceptance affect the person being received?

- Without divine resources we can't extend or receive the kind of acceptance we just considered. And instead we hide conflict behind *congeniality;* we rechannel it into *cooperation* on a worthy project; or we find *consolation* to soothe the pain we feel. If the conflict is severe, we work through our issues in *counseling* or we let *conforming* pressures try to contain our ugliness within renewed efforts to do better. Review the chart on page 41. Which of your current relationships fall into each of the five categories listed beneath "Conflicted Relationships" under "Unspiritual Community," relationships that we develop in order to handle conflict? As you look at your lists, consider whether you long for more—and what that "more" might be.

No one knows or is known by another without entering more fully into God's presence. The resources for connecting with each other must be given to us by the Spirit and nourished by yielding to Him as much as Mary did in order to conceive. Spiritual community depends on spiritual resources, but so much of our community time is unspiritual. In the next chapter, Dr. Crabb asks what makes unspiritual community unspiritual and looks more closely at the five kinds of relationships that we sometimes assume are spiritual.

CHAPTER 6
Why Unspiritual Community
Is Unspiritual

- Look again at the opening account of Dr. Crabb's interaction with his friend. Describe what Dr. Crabb did. What did you learn from his response to his friend—and, in turn, his friend's response? In what relationship(s) could you follow his example and offer prayer rather than interpretations, advice, or attempts to fix the situation?

- Dr. Crabb believes that the root of all nonmedical human struggle is really a spiritual problem, a disconnection from God that creates a disconnection from oneself and from others. That disconnection consists of a determination to take care of oneself in the face of a disappointing and sometimes assaultive world where we conclude that no one exists who has our best interests at heart. That's unbelief. The resolve to look after oneself (call that *rebellion*) breaks fellowship with God and others and involves a violation of our created nature to be givers (disconnection from self). Does this diagnosis fit your personal struggles, past or present? The struggles of people you know? Would it fit the person involved in a divorce? A person addicted to pornography? A person dealing with an incestuous childhood? Explain why you answered yes or no in each case.

- In community, our determination to fully trust no one must die and an eager willingness to receive what is best from others and to give what is best from within ourselves must take its place. That only happens when people feel loved, safe, trusting, and courageous—and still it requires a risk. When, if ever, have you risked being fully known—or at least more fully known—by another person? If so, what happened? What lessons did you learn about yourself . . . about God . . . about community? If you haven't taken that risk, what road-blocks stand in your path?

- Review the discussion of "Conflicted Community," specifically the comments of the apostle James, Ashley Montagu, Charlotte Buhler, Abraham Maslow, and Dr. Crabb. What points were especially significant to you? As you consider the source of conflict, with which perspective do you most agree? Why? In your view, is the drive toward self-actualization good or bad? Explain.

- When our agendas directly compete with someone else's self-occupied agenda, conflict erupts, and we too easily depend on one of five kinds of relationship to handle the conflict, none of which belong to spiritual community. Look again at the description of each (pages 53–56). What weakness(es) do you find in each type of relationship? Put differently, how does each contradict your idea of spiritual, biblical community?

- The final five paragraphs of this chapter are filled with vision and hope. What do you find most appealing about what Dr. Crabb says here? Most challenging?

Psychologists C. H. Patterson and Suzanne Hidore propose that the essence of all successful psychotherapy is love, but Dr. Crabb is disturbed by the idea of purchasing love via therapy. But we have turned to professionals because spiritual community is rare. We offer congenial, cooperative, consoling, counseling, and conforming relationships to people in conflict. Can we do better?

PART II

A Way of Understanding Our Struggles

CHAPTER 7
Two
Rooms

- Review the discussion of the two rooms (see pages 61–65 and the bulleted lists on pages 67, 69) and then briefly describe the two rooms in your own words. Why are "Upper" and "Lower" appropriate designations even though they aren't spatially accurate? In response to the first list, identify evidence that you are living like a citizen of the Lower Room. Then identify which aspect(s) of the Upper Room makes it most appealing.

- Dr. Crabb describes the furnishings in the Lower Room: (1) We long for good relationships; (2) we look after our own needs; (3) our worlds frustrate and satisfy us, sometimes more one than the other; (4) we learn what we like and go after it; and (5) we are aware of a moral code that tells us what we should or should not do in our pursuit of happiness. Lower Rooms also often contain hard memories of, as in Sheila's case, an alcoholic father and clinging mother. What percentage of your time are you living in your Lower Room? What influences try to keep you there? What hard memories keep you there? How, if at all, do you try to merely add God to this room? Describe your level of success.

- C. S. Lewis once said that if we discover desires within us that nothing in this world can satisfy, we really should wonder if we were designed for another world. When, if ever, have you recognized such desires within you? Describe such a moment. What does this observation by Lewis suggest about the two rooms?

- Despite occasional and momentary dissatisfaction with the Lower Room, many people live there quite happily for a long time. They see no value in brokenness and radical trust because their resources are keeping life together quite well, and the unspiritual community of congenial, cooperative, comforting, counseling, and conforming relationships seems to work. When, if ever, have you been forced to admit that true life and true community and true joy are not available in the Lower Room that for so long you have called home? What circumstances and/or realizations contributed to that admission?

- Read again Dr. Crabb's letter to Sheila, imagining this time that he's writing to you. What encouragement do you find there? What specific points of application will you try for yourself?

To change rooms, to hear the Spirit speak through God's Word to us, to enjoy communion with Christ and sense the Father's presence, and then to speak from that room into the reality of our difficult lives, two things need to happen. One, we need to see our Lower Room for what it is and, two, we need to join a church, to become part of a community of people on a journey to God. In the next two chapters, Dr. Crabb further describes the Lower Room, hoping to help you both see it for what it is and then feel an excited desperateness to find a man carrying water who can lead you to your Upper Room.

CHAPTER 8
There Is a
Lower Room

- The chapter opens with Dr. Crabb's perhaps startling statement "I have had moments when I wondered if my faith would survive." What situations in your life have threatened your trust in God? What kept you anchored in your faith despite the pain and confusion—or, if you did fall away for a season, what brought you back?

- Seeing in three people the forces of wretchedness overcome in substantial measure by the forces of greatness helped Dr. Crabb stay anchored in his faith. Name someone in your life who has known dishonor or heartbreak that exposed their feet of clay, yet from whom a seemingly indestructible and uncorrupted life radiates. What correlation have you seen between excruciatingly difficult trials and compelling faith in Jesus?

- Wretchedness, our own wretchedness, must be recognized not only as a past reality but also as a present reality. Why do we—individually as well as corporately—fail to see our wretchedness? Why do we balk at acknowledging it? Why do we downplay, if not totally ignore, our wretchedness? Give five or six reasons in answer to these three questions.

- Review Pascal's quote (pages 77-78) as another step toward getting rid of the idea that wretchedness is evidence of complexity (rather than unholiness or wickedness) or psychological disturbance (as opposed to sin) and that greatness is the manageable product of good training, economic advantage, or, if necessary, therapy. Then, as a further step toward acknowledging your wretchedness, cite from your own life a behavior or a comment that is an example of a hybrid of Lower and Upper Room energy (see pages 75–76) for Dr. Crabb's example).

- Dr. Crabb offers an overview both of our current culture (pages 76–77) and of the history that brought us to our present level of morality (pages 77–79). What points that he made were new, striking, and/or alarming?

Whatever is wrong with us destroys relationships and makes spiritual community impossible. Until we recover a distinctly Christian view of this wretchedness—that lies beneath eating disorders and multiple personalities and sexual addictions and relational conflict—the value of spiritual community will not be recognized. But along with a depth view of moral wretchedness, we must also recover a rich understanding of universal priesthood in the church. We're all priests, we all have direct access to God and can draw near to Him, and we all have the life of the Spirit within us waiting to be poured into others. And it is that life that can heal the soul.

CHAPTER 9
Lower Room
Furnishings

- C. S. Lewis makes a distinction between solid people and ghosts. Solid people have given up whatever idols they had depended on to give them life, and that surrendering doesn't come without suffering. Suffering brings into focus what one's soul most deeply yearns for and a person is directed to God. Dr. Crabb tells of a time when he was a ghost (pages 82–83). When have you met an unsafe ghost? When have you been an unsafe ghost? In both cases be specific in your description and your analysis of what lay behind the ghostlike quality.

- Lower Room, cesspool, flesh, snakes, cellar sins—each description fits. How did you respond as you read about these aspects of yourself? What did God show you about yourself through these descriptions?

- Review the statements of Henri Nouwen (page 81), C. S. Lewis (pages 81 and 85), and Richard Lovelace commenting on Jonathan Edwards (pages 83–84). What better understanding of the Lower Room did each offer you? What phrases were especially striking or convicting?

- Dr. Crabb confesses a time when he entered the ring and knocked out his Animal Self but had not seen his Diabolical Self sitting ringside and grinning broadly. As he said, "The snakes were crawling, the stench from the cesspool was rising—and I thought I had just splashed on some cologne." Be specific about a similar experience of one of your own cellar sins.

• Look again at the four furnishings of our Lower Room. Review the more detailed descriptions as well (pages 87–94).

— The corrupted *image* of God that fills us with a *passion* for *self*

— The corrupted *resources* we've been given as human beings that fill us with a *passion* for *control*

— Pleasurable and painful *life experiences* that we corrupt by responding to them with a *passion* to *define* life (pleasures we must reexperience) and death (pain we must avoid)

— The corruption of *God's holy law* that was given to reveal our need but now stimulates a *passion* to *perform* that literally drives us mad

What action, statement, and/or attitude during the last week did God call to mind as you read the descriptions of these furnishings either initially or just now? Which sinful passion—for self, control, definition, or performance—do you most grapple with? In your own words, why are the smell of the cesspool and the sense of serpents crawling up your legs valuable to your own walk with the Lord and essential to spiritual community?

The passion for self ("Give me what I need"), the passion for control ("I'll make it happen"), the passion to define ("This is life, and this is death"), and the passion to perform ("I'll try to be good, but can't You just let me do what I want?") are what Dr. Crabb calls "flesh dynamics," our effort to become solid, whole persons without God. And these dynamics are the smelly cesspool, the slithering serpents. How can we build spiritual community with these passions ruling our lives? We can't. But God has a plan that can lead us to spiritual community. . . .

CHAPTER 10
There *Is* an
Upper Room

- "A Christian world-view provides reason to respect each other, to expect to learn from every encounter with a fellow image bearer. Only in Christianity is there a clear basis for regarding each other as having profound worth." Explain the basis for this respect and regard. Use Scripture if you'd like.

- Spiritual community is always a miracle because we all have people in our lives—people like Peggy, Marshall, Marlene, Gary, Suzanne, and Mel—in whom we struggle to see the Upper Room. Which small group experiences or individuals came to mind as you read about these folks? Give several examples and make that list of people a focus of a prayer of confession as you ask God to transform not only your heart but your perspective on these people He created, some of whom He has welcomed into His family because of their faith in His Son. Spiritual community never happens without the Spirit, so pray for God's Spirit to be active within you and yield yourself to His work.

- We are all too prone to "connect" with others from our Lower Room and to see only that room in others, a fact that makes marriage quite challenging. As Dr. Crabb says of his own marriage, "Perhaps our greatest battle, and at the same time our richest blessing, has been to see the Upper Room in each other." Thinking about your spouse or a close friend, describe the benefits of focusing on the Upper Room and the damage done by connecting from your Lower Room.

- Dr. Crabb writes, "When I believe that you believe I am a good man, I don't tend toward arrogance or presumption. I rest. And in my rest I am more able to face my Diabolical Self and to then discover and celebrate my Celestial Self. . . . I know of little else so powerful as confessing wretched failing and having a friend look on you with great delight." Who in your life has offered or offers you this kind of rest? Why do neither arrogance nor presumption tend to result from such acceptance? To whom are you able to offer such delight and acceptance despite a wretchedness that isn't hidden?

- In spiritual community, Dr. Crabb asserts, "the overriding focus in a spiritual conversation is not sin or psychological damage but the Spirit's movement. What's good? What evidence can we find of the Spirit's creative involvement in each other's life?" In what upcoming interaction or ongoing relationship will you try to keep this perspective? Start now by considering evidence of the Spirit's work in his/her life. Write down specifics about what you see.

Because of people in our life who see our Upper Room—who see the healthy tissue mixed in with the bad, the principle of greatness at work even when the principle of wretchedness is far more visible—we can sometimes feel safe. Thanks to how they see me, I more deeply know that I am in Christ and I more fully know that Christ is in me, that beneath every base desire there is a robust appetite for holiness. Only when these truths are positioned in our minds will an overwhelming revelation of the depths of our depravity provoke not despair but worship.

CHAPTER 11
Upper Room
Furnishings

- The chapter opens with an invitation to think of someone who right now is worrying you. Dr. Crabb asks you to think truthfully, accurately, realistically. You've seen that person's Lower Room. Were you able, as you did the exercise, to see the Upper Room? Describe that experience—or do the exercise now and comment on the effects of looking for and seeing that person's Upper Room. Who tends to see your Upper Room despite his or her familiarity with your Lower Room? What does that kind of acceptance do for you?

- Review the overview of biblical, covenant history on pages 106–11. What new insight—or what new appreciation for knowledge you already had—did you gain from this account?

- What seems to be most overlooked in all the blessings brought on by the New Covenant is that it makes possible a new way to relate. Dr. Crabb lists these four provisions of the covenant:

  — A new purity: We receive forgiveness so complete that it's hard to actually grasp.

  — A new identity: We're now saints who sin, not hopeless sinners.

  — A new inclination: We want to do good.

  — A new power: God's Spirit within us releases the same power that raised Jesus from the dead, enabling us to obey and love.

- If you're a believer, describe your experience of each. If you have not yet committed your life to Christ, which provision is most appealing to you? Why? (Committing your life to Christ requires an acknowledgment of your sinfulness and a request for forgiveness as you name Jesus your Savior and Lord. The prayer can be simple: "Dear God, I realize how much I fall short of Your holiness. . . . I confess my sinfulness . . . and ask Your forgiveness. . . . Thank You for sending Your Son, Jesus, to die on the cross for my sins. I humbly accept that great sacrifice, and, Jesus, I ask You now to be my Savior and my Lord. Amen.")

- The four provisions of the New Covenant correspond to the four furnishings of the Upper Room, which Dr. Crabb identifies as follows:

  1. The renewed image of Christ with its *passion* to *worship*

  2. A recognition of who we are and who God is that stirs a *passion* to *trust*

  3. An attitude toward life experiences that views them as an opportunity to satisfy a *passion* to *grow*

  4. An embracing of God's law as the character of the Person we most love that fuels a *passion* to *obey*

- Review the descriptions of each passion (pages 112–17). What action, statement, and/or attitude during the last week did God call to mind as you read the descriptions of these furnishings either initially or just now? Or, put more simply, which of these passions have you had a taste of in the last week? What prompted that moment of passion? Which passion—to worship, trust, grow, and obey— most regularly guides you? Explain in your own words why each of these passions is valuable to your own walk with the Lord and contributes to spiritual community.

- Look again at the chart on pages 116–17. What do you now more clearly understand about struggles and how best to deal with them? About the role that spiritual community can play in your struggles?

Now turn to "The Tasks of Spiritual Community" listed on page 118. What do you find inviting and especially worthwhile about that description?

In the book of Hebrews, the writer reminds us that the New Covenant is better than the old one in every way. With the blessings of our new purity, our new identity, our new inclinations, and our new power, we can draw near to God and to each other in new ways. And then he instructs us to make sure we keep getting together as a new covenant community and, when we do, to think hard about how we can arouse the passions of the Upper Room, how we can stir each other's desire to love and do good into a consuming fire. So next, in Part III, we will look at what we can do to build spiritual community, to become a community of people on a journey to God that is the safest place on earth for everything good to happen.

PART III

A Way of Relating
in This World

CHAPTER 12

Turning Our Souls toward Each Other:
Three Fundamental Convictions

- What interferes with your desire to worship, trust, grow, and obey? What interferes with your efforts to do those things?

- The Lower Room is not razed with salvation. Therefore the good passions to worship, trust, grow, and obey are often weak and hard to find. But what indications have you had that those good passions lie within your heart? Your specific evidence may not be as dramatic as the friend with the bad arm, but then again it just might be. "When those passions in me meet those same passions in you," Dr. Crabb writes, "we experience spiritual community." Are those indications that good passions exist clearer when you're with a fellow believer? In worship? If you answered yes, why might that be so?

- This chapter outlines three convictions that need to be believed firmly and strongly if we are to turn our chairs completely enough for our souls to meet. As surely as birds were made to fly and fish to swim, we were made for community, for the kind of community the Trinity enjoys, for *spiritual* community. And to the degree we experience it, we change, we grow, we heal. Foundational Conviction #1 is that spiritual community is the work of the Spirit, not our work. Review the discussion of this conviction (pages 125–28). When have you seen—or come closest to seeing—that without the Spirit and the Christ He represents, you can do nothing of real value? And when have you seen in your life or the life of someone close to you that, as God teaches us to depend on Him, we may struggle for years against small problems but He supplies the power to conquer big problems quickly? Next, our most difficult work in forming spiritual community is to stop working so hard. Why is this difficult? Finally, what role does prayer play in the development of spiritual community?

- Foundational Conviction #2 is that the quality of the energy that comes out of us—energy for good or for bad—depends on our level of fellowship with God. When have you seen the quality of your impact on people be impacted by the degree of your fellowship with God? Give a few specific examples. In light of the personal experiences you just shared, look again at Peter Kreeft's comments (page 128). Do you agree or disagree? Why? Then, again, what role does prayer play in the development of spiritual community?

- Foundational Conviction #3 is that having a safe place to own and trace our desires to their source will put us in touch with our hunger for God. Too often the distractions of busyness have sealed us off from what we most desire. Fear can also form a moat around our soul. Does a moat surround your soul? If so, what alligators of distractions and/or addictions have you filled it with? James Houston says, "The unsatisfied longing for God is what drives human beings above all else." Do you agree or disagree? Why? What seems to be driving you? Spend some time considering whether that desire is a meager expression of your deepest desire to know God.

We need a safe place to admit and explore our desires, a community of fellow journeyers who believe that our desires are not at root shameful but thoroughly human and already met in Jesus. We need a place to feel safe enough to meaningfully explore who we are with confidence that the end point would be a joyful meeting with God. These three convictions will help us move toward that goal as we build on them an approach to developing spiritual community.

CHAPTER 13
The Fork in the Road to
Spiritual Community

- Review the opening account of a significant interaction that a discouraged Dr. Crabb had with a friend. Look closely at the conversation and Dr. Crabb's analysis of what was happening, what God was doing through his friend. What is striking about the conversation? About the analysis? When has a friend helped you, as C. S. Lewis said, discover God?

- Why is *the passion to celebrate* (defined on pages 136–37), which grows out of a New Purity, healing? Put differently, why does an acknowledgment of sin lead to worship? When have you had a taste of this? Who, if anyone, celebrates you—or whom do you celebrate despite an awareness of that person's Lower Room?

- Why is *the passion to envision* (defined and discussed on pages 137–38) an antidote to the sinful passion to control and therefore healing? Explain in your own words why the passion to envision stirs the passion to trust God. When has the experience of finally relinquishing to God your apparent control of something helped you grow in your trust of Him? Be specific. The passion to trust that stirs in each saint, kindled by the provision of a New Identity, translates into the passion to envision what the other is becoming as we journey together. What do you envision for the people you're close to? Who "envisions" for you—and what is that person's impact on your life? What might it mean to be part of a community of "envisioners"?

• *The passion to discern* (discussed on pages 138–39) arises from the New Covenant gift of a new disposition. When have you found yourself actually preferring holiness . . . feeling a deep passion to grow . . . welcoming trials as a means of spiritual formation? Be specific about each. Why is it healing to view suffering not as an enemy? When have you responded—or seen someone respond—to pain as an opportunity for growth? What growth happened? (It may be too early to answer that question.) What impact did the expectation of or openness to growth have on the person suffering?

• *The passion to empower* (discussed on pages 139–40) represents a movement away from feeling pressure. Why is that movement a step of healing? When have you experienced at least a taste of the passion to obey? The passion to obey excited by the Holy Spirit who is our New Power translates into a passion to give to others whatever the Spirit rouses in us so that they will be further stirred to obey our Lord. We actually present Christ to each other when we freely offer whatever is most spiritually alive in us. When have you been presented with Christ in another person? Describe that experience and how it moved you toward holiness.

• Spiritual community heals the soul by releasing into someone passions that lift that person into the Upper Room. From there, Lower Room passions are exposed for the sin that they are. But those Lower Room passions must be seen before we will disregard them. Only seeing better passions that are solid and noble frees us to recognize evil passions for what they are. Look again at the chart on page 142, the climactic conclusion to the chapter, and the questions raised in the four paragraphs that follow. In you own words, define the fork in the road, the choice that Dr. Crabb presents here. What fear, hesitation, excitement, and/or anticipation do you feel as you consider choosing being a mystic over being a manager? Be specific—and prayerful.

Spiritual community can be thought of as an exchange between two or more people that reflects four passions: the safety of celebration, the hope of vision, the wisdom of loving discernment, and the power of touch. The community is spiritual if the passions aroused in us as we meet with each other are the direct and supernatural effect of living in the reality of what God has provided in the New Covenant. The fork in the road represents the broad path of continuing on as managers, of trying to develop healing communities while we remain in the Lower Room. It also presents the narrow path of becoming mystics, people who experience the presence and the movement of God within their soul. The rest of the book suggests what is required to choose the path of mysticism.

CHAPTER 14
Managers or Mystics:
The Mystery of Community

- A safe community where souls can heal is a community where people look at one another and are stirred by the Spirit to experience holy passions. Out of those passions they speak, and passions are not easily managed. So we put ourselves in the humble position of dependence on God: We become mystics. Dr. Crabb defines *mysticism* as "the felt arousal of spiritual passions within the regenerate heart, passions that can have no existence apart from a Spirit-revealed knowledge of truth and the promptings of the same Spirit to enjoy that truth." How is this definition different from your earlier understanding of mysticism? What do you find appealing, intriguing, or even threatening about this definition?

- The difficulty is that we're either managers or bad mystics. We tend to feel all the wrong passions. Dr. Crabb gives a personal example of feeling all the wrong passions. In what recent situation from your own life would you have rather felt the high passions? When was your Diabolical Self—your concern for self, for being in control, for avoiding pain, for succumbing to pressure to do right—released despite perhaps an external appearance of graciousness?

- The starting point for spiritual community to develop is not learning and practicing relational skills; it is relating with God, drawing near to Him through the door opened by the New Covenant. In what ways are you—and/or could you be—taking advantage of the door opened by the Cross? What, for instance, are you doing to put yourself in a position for learning the humility of giving up power over others?

• The spirituality of a community can be measured not merely by its doctrinal statement but by the passions that are most deeply aroused. Look in the mirror and, whether you answer yes or no, give evidence to support your answer to each of the following questions.

— Is your passion for worship elbowing out your passion for self?

— Does your passion to trust nudge aside your passion to control?

— Does your passion to grow make you willing to suffer whatever pain is needed?

— Is your passion to obey relieving the pressure to do something right and instead causing you to delight with anything you do right?

— Are you afraid of mystery?

— Are you afraid of the Holy Spirit?

• What new perspective on heaven did you gain from the discussion on page 151? And what new or renewed hope for spiritual community do you find in 2 Peter 1:3–4?

At this point, perhaps a model that loosely captures a strategy for becoming a mystical community, for developing the safest place on earth, will help. But first we must make sure we are willing to move toward spiritual community. There is a price.

CHAPTER 15
It's Worth
the Risk

- When in your life has it been easier to believe in a watchmaker who started the clock ticking and then backed away than in a sovereign, loving God who could make things better and didn't? And when in your life have you wished you—metaphorically—had never gone to see the doctor, that you had never tried to reveal more of yourself and be more intimate with another person, much less with a community of people?

- Dr. Crabb invites you to look around. Do the happiest people you know seem to be the least involved in substantive, deeply personal community? What do you make of that appearance, of that apparent reality? Why could this be the case?

- Dr. Crabb writes, "The dangers of community seem better to me than the dull safety of independence. Only what is bad is endangered in spiritual community." Based on your growing understanding of spiritual community, identify what that "bad" might be and then explain whether you agree or disagree with this statement and why.

- Dr. Crabb openly shares his fears about his quest for spiritual community, saying that he wonders if his quest is like Dorothy's search for Oz or like Don Quixote's tilting at windmills in a crusade that has no point. Do you have such thoughts about yourself? Equally as important, do you—having gotten a glimpse of the glories of the temple—share Dr. Crabb's excitement about what spiritual community could be? What can keep you (and Dr. Crabb) from settling for less?

- In your journey to God, He will take you to a point where a choice among three options must be made—going mad, backing up, or journeying on (page 159). Suggest what could prompt a person to make each choice and then list the advantages and disadvantages of each option. Which option are you leaning toward? Why?

In any serious attempt to build true community, we will wrestle with confusion, disappointment, and, occasionally, excruciating agony of soul. Those struggles will compel us to fix our eyes on unseen reality—the Spirit is at work—and to believe in a better day ahead—Christ is coming back.

CHAPTER 16
ENTER, SEE, TOUCH:
A Way of Developing Spiritual Community

- Look again at the first three pages of the chapter and then explain in your own words why spiritual community begins with brokenness.

- Before presenting his vision of the pathway to spiritual community, Dr. Crabb reminds those in spiritual leadership that everything— evangelism, discipleship, youth ministry, *everything*—flows from worship. He also states that he views the preaching/worship service as a preparation for community, as a prelude to journeying more closely together in the right direction. The point of church is journeying together to God. Is yours a worshiping community? If you answer yes, give specific evidence; if you answer no, share your ideas about how your church could be more worshipful. When, if ever, has your experience of worship paved the way for greater intimacy or closer community with a fellow believer?

- Spiritual community is always a miracle. It cannot be programmed into existence. It must be prayed into existence. And we so easily pray for what we know we cannot control and work on what we still think we can control. Summarize the value of prayer and waiting in relation to the development of spiritual community. What lesson does Henri Nouwen draw from the life of Christ? When have your or your church's efforts at ministry and perhaps efforts to develop spiritual community been backward from Christ's model? What might have been different had you followed His example?

- Spiritual community begins with prayer. The next step involves laying the foundation based on three essential convictions (growth is a mystery; personal holiness counts for more than trained skill; and every felt desire is, at root, a longing for God, though often unrecognized as such) and on a solid grasp of God's truth as revealed in Jesus Christ (truth that gives rise to spiritual passions for worship, trust, growth, and obedience; New Testament truth with its provisions for a new purity, new identity, new disposition, and new power). Review the four numbered statements, the flow chart, and the three bulleted points where Dr. Crabb pulls together everything he has said so far in the book (pages 168–70). What light bulbs went on for you as you read this section? What excitement was kindled or further inflamed? What will you do with these new insights about, and stirred desires for, spiritual community?

- Enter, see, touch—consider now whether you are ready to take these steps and whether you've already had a taste of what each means.

  — *Enter.* Dr. Crabb will let you into his soul if you are broken yet strong, vulnerable with hope, and respectfully curious. Do you qualify? Be specific. Is there any broken person in your life who feels his/her neediness but whose strength you feel; who always finds a reason to worship God and to celebrate you; and who can say hard things to you and you appreciate it? What enables a person to be like that?

  — *See.* What is the difference between envisioning and discerning, and, in spiritual community, how do the two complement each other? In whom do you see some facet of Christ—and what facet do you see? Who seems to see a facet of Christ in you—and what facet is that? Who in your life seems especially sensitive to the Spirit's present and immediate activity? In what ways do you benefit from contact with that person? When, if ever, has someone commented on God's Spirit at work in or through you?

What kind of community or communion with that person did you sense at the time?

— *Touch.* A wise friend of Dr. Crabb once said, "Christ always leads gently." Be specific about a time when the Lord clearly but gently led you. When has the Lord clearly led you through a fellow member of Christ's body? When, if ever, has someone let you know that the Lord used you to lead him/her? How did these experiences affect your relationship with that person?

• If you merely read through the last section of the chapter (beginning on page 173), this time read the words and then follow the suggestions. If you are not already in a small group, consider your spouse, a prayer partner, or a close friend whom you see regularly as you work through the four steps.

Spiritual community develops as the passions of God's Spirit, aroused by the truth of the gospel, begin to flow between people as they relate. Don't stop getting together, and when you are together, think hard about how to stimulate one another to love and do good deeds. It's time to turn our chairs toward one another.

CHAPTER 17
Becoming
Spiritual Community

- When have God's people—or one of God's people—been a rock in stormy seas for you? What impact did that experience have on you—on your faith, your pain, your circumstances, your strength? What if you had been able to turn to a genuine spiritual community as defined by Dr. Crabb in this book?

- Define what you understand Dr. Crabb to mean by the phrase "spiritual direction." How is that different from what modern psychology offers?

- Competence to care for souls and to cure them, to nurture the work of the Spirit in another's life, depends first on spiritual maturity, on the depth of the helper's communion with God. Who in your life might qualify for this role? When have you worked with—or when have you considered working with—a counselor or therapist? What problem or pain were you facing? Was the psychological problem fundamentally a spiritual one? What would a spiritual director have offered that you didn't receive or wouldn't have received?

- Read Maria's story again. In your own words explain how she would benefit from the guidance of a spiritual director and from involvement in a genuine spiritual community.

- Now look at your own life. How would it be different if you were involved in a genuine spiritual community? What will you do to find a spiritual community like the one Dr. Crabb has been describing?

The church needs many things. It will properly prioritize its needs only when it gets its purpose straight. Its purpose is to draw people into Christ, to mirror Christ to one another, to show Christ to others by the way we live. That happens only in a community of people on a journey to God, only in a group of people who turn their chairs toward each other. If such a community is appealing to you, Dr. Crabb invites you to join him in prayer to hear the mind of God, to see what He would have you do. The church is a community of spiritual friends and spiritual directors who journey together to God. We must become that community. Prayer is the starting point.

Notes

Chapter 1

1. See Alistair McGrath, *Evangelicalism and the Future of Christianity* (Downers Grove, IL: InterVarsity Press, 1995), 55–56, for a list of "six controlling convictions" that define evangelical orthodoxy, convictions I believe without reservation.

2. I am indebted to Dr. Richard Averbeck, Old Testament professor at Trinity Evangelical Divinity School, for this term. My apologies to him if I misuse it.

Chapter 2

1. See Henri Nouwen, *Sabbatical Journey* (New York: Crossroad, 1998), 25. "What to do with this inner wound that is so easily touched and starts bleeding again? I don't think this wound—this immense need for affection, and this immense fear of rejection—will ever go away. It is there to stay, but maybe for a good reason. Perhaps it is a gateway to my salvation, a door to glory, and a passage to freedom."

2. *Story of a Soul: The Autobiography of St. Therese of Lisieux,* trans. John Clarke (Washington, DC: ICS Publications, 1996).

Chapter 3

1. If there is authentic spiritual movement, it will be in both of us. If I pour something into him that moves him toward Christ, I will be similarly moved, maybe more. It *is* more blessed to give than receive. No one leaves a moment of spiritual community unaffected.

2. I first introduced this distinction between a *goal* (what we must have and no one but ourselves can block) and a *desire* (what we badly want but may not get) in an earlier book, *The Marriage Builder* (Grand Rapids, MI: Zondervan, 1982).

Chapter 4

1. Jean Vanier, *From Brokenness to Community* (New York: Paulist Press, 1993), 26–27.

Chapter 5

1. Maggie Ross, *The Fire of Your Life: A Solitude Shared* (San Francisco, CA: HarperSanFrancisco, 1992), 120.
2. Ibid., 3.
3. Quoted in Richard Foster, *Devotional Classics* (London: Hodder & Stoughton, 1993), 441.

Chapter 6

1. C. H. Patterson and Suzanne Hidore, *Successful Psychotherapy: A Caring, Loving Relationship* (Northvale, NJ: Jason Aranson, 1997), see chapter 1.
2. Ibid., xv, 1–22.
3. Ibid., 13.
4. Quoted in Patterson and Hidore, *Successful Psychotherapy*, 26.
5. Ibid., 26.
6. Ibid., 26.
7. Ibid., 26.

Chapter 7

1. Quoted in Richard Foster, *Devotional Classics* (London: Hodder & Stoughton, 1993), 478.
2. Ibid., 479.
3. See Galatians 5:16–23.

Chapter 8

1. All three quotations appeared in "A New Tale for Presidents' Day," *USA Today,* 12 February 1999, p. 5A.
2. Quoted in Foster, *Devotional Classics,* 253.
3. Ibid.

Chapter 9

1. Henri Nouwen, *Sabbatical Journey* (New York: Crossroad, 1998), 219–20.
2. Richard Lovelace, *Dynamics of Spiritual Life* (Downers Grove, IL: InterVarsity Press, 1979), 89.
3. Ibid., 86.
4. Teresa of Avila, *Interior Castle,* 3rd ed. (New York: Image Books, Doubleday, 1989), 40–41.
5. C. S. Lewis, *Mere Christianity* (New York: Macmillan, 1952), 94–95.

Chapter 10

1. Nouwen, *Sabbatical Journey,* 220.
2. Thomas à Kempis, *The Imitation of Christ* (London: Penguin Books, 1952), 45.

Chapter 11

1. Teresa of Avila, *Interior Castle,* 28.
2. I am indebted to the excellent teaching of Dwight Edwards, senior pastor of Grace Bible Church, College Station, Texas, for much of what I present in this section.
3. Robert Webber, *Worship Old and New* (Grand Rapids, MI: Zondervan, 1994), 31.
4. Everyone, I believe, harbors a secret fantasy to throw restraint to the wind and recklessly sin. It can sound so attractive. Those who don't yield fall into two classes: those who are afraid to and those

whose passion to trust is stronger. Those in the second group are the greater miracles.

Chapter 12

1. Teresa of Avila, *Interior Castle,* 47.
2. Quoted in a personal letter from a friend. I have not been able to trace the source in Peterson's writings.
3. Eugene Peterson from a friend's letter.
4. Peter Kreeft, *Christianity for Modern Pagans: Pascal's Pensees* (San Francisco: Ignatius Press), 321.
5. Ibid., 322.
6. James Houston, *The Heart's Desire* (Colorado Springs: NavPress, 1996), 21.
7. Ibid., 54.

Chapter 13

1. A. W. Tozer, *The Christian Book of Mystical Verse* (Harrisburg, PA: Christian Publications, 1963), vi.

Chapter 14

1. Quoted in Tozer, *The Christian Book of Mystical Verse,* 26–27.
2. Houston, *The Heart's Desire,* 17.
3. Ibid., 198.
4. Kreeft, *Christianity for Modern Pagans,* 236. Pascal then added, "If we offend the principles of reason, our religion will be absurd and ridiculous. Two excesses: to exclude reason, to admit nothing but reason" (p. 237).

Chapter 16

1. Tozer, *The Christian Book of Mystical Verse,* vii.
2. Wayne Martindale and Jerry Root, eds., *The Quotable Lewis* (Wheaton, IL: Tyndale, 1989).